Smash!

Moments, Memories, and Tips

by Dan Seemiller

©2021

Edited by Larry Hodges

INTRODUCTION

Table Tennis is one of the Summer Olympic sports one can play for a lifetime. If you like racket sports, and learn the fundamentals correctly, this sport will bring you many years of memories, challenges, and friends. Table Tennis is one of the best family sports there is. You can play at home with friends, at rec centers, or you can try your skill at the local table tennis club.

How I got started is the most common question I'm asked. Our local recreation center, Philips Park, had two tables. I played there regularly at ages 10 & 11. Then our parents bought our family a table for Christmas. With five brothers and three sisters, the table was pinging and ponging downstairs in the basement regularly. Practicing with my brothers and participating at South Park TT Club in Pittsburgh is how my table tennis career began.

The nearly 300 pictures on these pages are from a lifetime of table tennis. I considered putting them in chronological order. However, when I think back on my table tennis career, I don't think chronologically; I jump about, from memory to memory. And so I've put the pages in that same nearly random fashion as we jump from year to year.

Thank you to my sponsors and supporters these many years. USA Table Tennis, Butterfly, South Park & South Bend TTC, Larry Hodges, Senoda, Si & Patty Wasserman, Dr. Bill Walk, and my two coaches, Dell Sweeris and Houshang Bozorgzadeh.

FOREWORD

I discovered USA Table Tennis (then called USTTA) in 1976, when I was 16. I'd been playing some neighborhood ping-pong with a cheap hardbat, with my thumb on the back of the racket and hitting everything with the other side. You know, basement style - except, as someone would later tell me, it was almost a Seemiller grip! Seemiller, you say? Who's this Seemiller guy?

The first table tennis club I went to was the New Carrollton TT Club in Maryland. The first thing I noticed there were the incredible players! They were like professionals - or, as I'd later learn, rated over 1800!!! *Wow!!!* But the second thing I saw, being the bookish type, was a *Table Tennis Topics* magazine someone had tossed aside, the national magazine for USTTA. I grabbed it and began browsing it. Someone pointed at a picture on page 5 and said, "That's Danny C. Miller, the best player in the United States." I looked at it, probably scrunching my eyebrows in confusion (and seeing in the caption that it

Photo by Don Weems
DANNY SEEMILLER, MIDDLESEX OPEN WINNER.

Here's the picture I saw from the March/April 1976 *Table Tennis Topics*. Danny C. Miller, dancing and yelling at the ball?

was "Seemiller" who had just won the Middlesex Open in England, a big international tournament), and asked, "What's he doing? It looks like he's dancing and yelling at the ball." The person laughed and said, "No, that's a backhand serve." So began my table tennis education and my introduction to Danny Seemiller. (They let me keep the magazine - and it's from the tattered remains of that very same one that I scanned the picture on this page.)

The first time I saw him, live and in person, was at the 1976 US Open in Philadelphia in July - and he was walking a player picket line with a protest sign about the extremely low prize money in the tournament, which he and many other top players were boycotting. He was a celebrity, a table tennis god, to be seen but not spoken to. I saw him there and at other tournaments, but kept my distance - what would the #1 US player want to do with an 1100 player? (*I got better!*) So I'd just spy from a distance when he played, even trying to copy his serve and attack game - but always from a distance.

And then I finally met him, at his five-day Seemiller camp in Pittsburgh in 1977. He came into the club with a huge cast on his leg - he'd badly sprained his ankle playing touch football just before the camp - tripping over future star Scott Boggan. So they'd put a huge, hard cast on the leg to immobilize it so that he'd still be able to hobble about and demonstrate. And more than that - he took on challenges during breaks, staggering about in that cast. I watched him beat the US #1 junior player, Rutledge Barry, winning the last point with a huge forehand loop - and following through off-balance to the side where he almost ran into me! That was a

4

memorable moment for me; for him, it was Tuesday. I would attend another five-day Seemiller camp in Pittsburgh in 1978, and another in Wilson, North Carolina in 1979, learning from all three of the Seemillers - Danny, Ricky, and Randy, as well as "honorary" Seemiller, Perry Schwartzberg.

I continued to move up in the sport. In 1990, Danny was elected president of USTTA, and in 1991 I was elected Vice President, and we've been working together on table tennis issues ever since. Also in 1991, with his brothers retired from coaching, Dan hired me as assistant coach for his summer camps, and again in 1992. I've since run over 100 training camps - but I learned how from Danny, and modeled much of my coaching camps after his.

So who is Danny? He's the consummate professional athlete and table tennis person. He's done it all - table tennis champion (five-time US Men's Singles Champion, #19 in the world), US national team coach at the Worlds and Olympics, USATT president, club president, tournament director of numerous 4-star tournaments and even a Nationals, table tennis ambassador all over the world, and the 2008 USATT Lifetime

Charlie Wuvanich and Danny Seemiller protesting at the 1976 US Open, the first time I saw Danny. (See page 19.)

Achievement Award recipient - by far the youngest ever, at age 53 at the time of his selection. But as he said at the time, "*I'm not through yet!*" - and one year later, at the age of 55, he would, unbelievably, win his *twelfth* Men's Doubles title at the US Nationals, by far the oldest ever to accomplish that - and he'd do it with Mark Hazinski, one of his own students!

Oh, and did I leave out author? He's written three table tennis books, all available on Amazon: "*Winning Table Tennis*" (how to play), "*Revelations of a Ping-Pong Champion*" (his autobiography), and now *Smash! Moments, Memories, and Tips* - his life in pictures. And so, like me so long ago, you too can spy on him, experiencing his 50+-year journey and many adventures through his eyes, with his thoughts on each picture. Plus, there's a table tennis tip on nearly every page!

Larry Hodges
USATT Hall of Famer
2018 USATT Lifetime Achievement Award Winner
USATT Certified National Coach
Student of Danny's

Tip: Make sure you follow through on your strokes. Here is a topspin loop in photo 1 and a smash in photo 2. The key to a quality stroke is that the backswing and follow through are even in length.

U. S. Men's and Women's Teams and their support group at the Syracuse National Sports Festival III. Jamie

The National Sports Festival was a very much looked forward to event in the 80s for America's up-and-coming players. Here's the group from Syracuse, N.Y. in 1981.

Tip: It's important to be a team player and be supportive no matter what your role in the team is. It's a great feeling to help a teammate out when they are down and vice versa.

National Championships

DANNY SEEMILLER　　　　**RICKY SEEMILLER**

Undefeated eight-time National Doubles Champions

Doubles is all about teamwork. Usually it is best for a lefty-righty pairing, with one player good at getting the attack and the other a finisher. With Rick and I, I was the setup man, and he would hit the more aggressive shots. Sometimes when Rick and I would play I would get frustrated as in photo 2. Here we had just returned from five weeks training in Japan and Rick was having a tough tourney. Whenever one trains overseas and you return, there are expectations and that can be a hard thing to overcome.

Tip: Serving short–2 bounces–is a common high level technique.

Swaythling Cup Records Of U.S. Players

Dan Seemiller		Matches W-L	Games W-L
		26-0	52-2
WON			
Omran	(Egy)		6,18
Sondol	(Egy)		9,12
Ezz	(Egy)		11,10
Krier	(Lux)		13,14
Hartman	(Lux)		14,12
Putz	(Lux)		8,18
Zikos	(Gr)		16,18
Christodoulatos	(Gr)		12,13
Priftis	(Gr)		18,17
Belien	(Bel)		4,10
VandeWalle	(Bel)		6,10
Nassaux	(Bel)		14,13
Cheng Kok Liong	(Mal)		9,13
Peong Tah Sung	(Mal)		16,7
Chen Scheng Shien	(HK)		12,-20,10
Vong Iu Veng	(HK)		12,20
Li Kuang Tsu	(HK)		10,7
McNee	(Scot)		9,7
Sutherland	(Scot)		8,7
Yule	(Scot)		12,8
Muller	(Aus)		15,11
Amplatz	(Aus)		18,15
Schluter	(Aus)		5,7
Constantini	(It)		14,9
Giontella	(It)		18,13
Bosi	(It)		-15,15,16

Ricky Seemiller		Matches W-L	Games W-L
		7-9	18-19
WON			
Peong Tah Seng	(Mal)		19,26
Lee Chung Kit	(Mal)		15,17
Vong Iu Veng	(HK)		19,18
Yule	(Scot)		17,16
McNee	(Scot)		17,17
Schluter	(Aus)		15,-11,16
Constantini	(It)		11,16
LOST			
Li Kuang Tsu	(HK)		-11,-15
Vong Iu Veng	(HK)		-14,15,-19
Hartman	(Lux)		18,-19,19
Putz	(Lux)		8,-12,-15
Krier	(Lux)		-14,-15
Li Kuang Tsu	(MK)		-11,16,-6
Amplatz	(Aus)		-18,-20
Giontella	(It)		-8,-10
Bosi	(It)		-7,-16

Ray Guillen		Matches W-L	Games W-L
		8-12	22-27
WON			
Omran	(Egy)		20,15
Sonbol	(Egy)		15,19
Christodoulatos	(Gr)		-17,15,14
Belien	(Bel)		11,13
Lee Chung Kit	(Mal)		18,-19,7
Vong Iu Veng	(MK)		19,9
Muller	(Aus)		19,-18,13
Giontella	(It)		13,16
LOST			
Schluter	(Aug)		-25,15,-16
Ezz	(Egy)		-15,-19
Priftis	(Gr)		-19,-18
Zikos	(Gr)		9,-22,-11
VandeWalle	(Bel)		-11,-17
Nassaux	(Bel)		-18,-9
Li Kuang Tsu	(HK)		-12,-15
Chen Scheng Shien	(HK)		-17,19,-19
Chen Scheng Shien	(HK)		8,-13,-13
Vong Iu Veng	(HK)		12,-14,-13
Constantini	(It)		14,-18,-13
Bosi	(It)		-18,-13

Dean Galardi		Matches W-L	Games W-L
		1-4	4-8
WON			
VandeWalle	(Bel)		15,17
LOST			
Sonbol	(Egy)		-19,-11
Ezz	(Egy)		-17,-19
Nassaux	(Bel)		16,-9,-18
Belien	(Bel)		18,-18,-12

Paul Raphael		Matches W-L	Games W-L
		1-7	5-15
WON			
Christodoulatos	(Gr)		19,-19,18
LOST			
Putz	(Lux)		-14,15,-16
Krier	(Lux)		-19,18,-11
Priftis	(Gr)		-18,-22
Zikos	(Gr)		-10,-15
Sutherland	(Scot)		-16,-14
Yule	(Scot)		-13,-18
Li Kuang Tsu	(HK)		15,-17,-9

TOTAL MATCHES W-L	TOTAL GAMES W-L
43-32	101-71

1977 was the breakthrough year that U.S. table tennis moved into the Elite Division at the World Championships. The team was myself, Rick, and three Californians: Dean Galardi, Ray Guillen, and Paul Raphel. We were down 4-2 to Italy and came back to win, 5-4.

Tip: If you want to be a good come-from-behind player then never give up. Fight to the end. Move your serve, try a different one. String a few points together and put pressure on your opponent.

Rick and I went on a worldwide trip in 1979. Starting in Pittsburgh, we went to Hong Kong for an Invitational, then to Tehran, Iran for some friendly matches, then back home, circling the globe. In Tehran, we played a match versus the National Team and beat them 3-0, but the match went quickly, and the Iranian team and the spectators wanted us to play again. After some financial negotiation we played and beat them again. This was one week before the hostage situation in 1979. We left just in time. Here is a photo of the U.S. and Iranian National teams at the 2008 Worlds in Guangzhou, China.

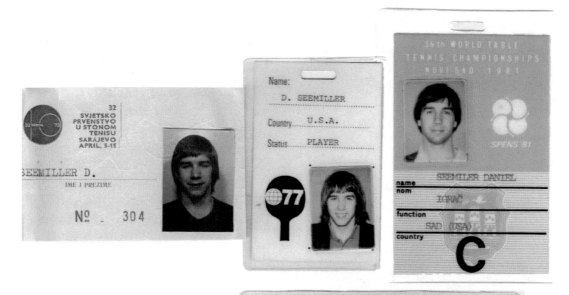

Raking through boxes of photos. Here's some of the ID tags over the years.

Kjell Johansson from Sweden, whose forehand was known as "The Hammer," shows us why he acquired that nickname. In the 1973 World Championships he was instrumental in Sweden winning the teams, and with Stellan Bengtsson won the Men's doubles and just barely lost in the singles final 3-2 21-18 to Hsi En-Ting. The last two points were edge balls.

Growing up in western Pennsylvania, I played many tournaments in Ohio, which was a TT hotbed in the 70s. I believe this one was in Columbus.

1st row: Sue Hildebrandt, Bill Lesner, Janice Martin, John Spencer behind Janice, John Temple, John Tannehill, Bert Jacobs, Me, and Mike Veillette

Sitting on right: Mike Dempsey

Back: Tim O'Grosky, Bill Hodge, and Manny Moskowitz

U.S. Swaythling Cup Record

Danny Seemiller (19-0)

WON

N. Thomas	(Wales)	4, 13
A. Griffiths	(Wales)	-16, 16, 14
D. Welsman	(Wales)	10, 15
M. Hafen	(Switz.)	12, 8
J. Barcikowski	(Switz.)	16, 13
T. Busin	(Switz.)	16, 16
C. L. Lim	(Mal.)	16, 9
K. Tay	(Mal.)	12, 15
B. S. Tan	(Mal.)	-16, 8, 12
A. Dewlatly	(Egy.)	16, 17
H. Sonbol	(Egy.)	13, 18
D. Palmi	(Austria)	11, 18
P. Gockner	(Austria)	6, 11
A. Vlieg	(Neth.)	-14, 9, 6
H. Gootzen	(Neth.)	-17, 13, 18
R. Hijne	(Neth.)	13, 17
S. Crisan	(Rum.)	15, 13
S. S. Chen	(H - K)	15, 13
M. K. Chiu	(H - K)	15, 16

Ricky Seemiller (8 - 6)

WON

M. Hafen	(Switz.)	18, 6
J. Barcikowski	(Switz.)	7, 7
B. S. Tan	(Mal.)	-17, 16, 15
E. Amplatz	(Austria)	16, 14
D. Palmi	(Austria)	18, 17
S. Dobosi	(Rum)	-10, 20, 19
S. Moraru	(Rum.)	16, 10
S. S. Chen	(H - K)	11, 14

LOST

T. Busin	(Switz.)	20, 20
K. Tay	(Mal.)	15, -16, -23
R. Hijne	(Neth.)	-14, -19
A. Vlieg	(Neth.)	-11, -10
H. Gootzen	(Neth.)	-14, -14
I. V. Vong	(H -K)	-15, -14

Scott Boggan (3 - 5)

WON

B. S. Tan	(Mal.)	-19, 17, 13
H. Sonbol	(Egy.)	10, 12
A. Meshref	(Egy.)	18, 22

LOST

C. L. Lim	(Mal.)	17, -20, -19
H. Gootzen	(Neth.)	-14, -14
R. Hijne	(Neth.)	-17, -19
J. Hansen	(Den.)	-18, -10
C. Pedersen	(Den.)	-8, -4

Eric Boggan (9 - 5)

WON

A. Griffiths	(Wales)	18, -6, 18
N. Thomas	(Wales)	22, 14
A. Meshref	(Egy.)	18, 12
P. Gockner	(Austria)	16, -9, 13
S. Moraru	(Rum.)	-17, 15, 12
S. Crisan	(Rum.)	-11, 16, 12
M. K. Chiu	(H - K)	17, 19
I. V. Vong	(H - K)	13, -19, 21
M. Daugard	(Den.)	-14, 14, 17

LOST

D. Welsman	(Wales)	14, -10, -14
J. Barcikowski	(Switz.)	10, -17, -5
T. Busin	(Switz.)	8, -12, -17
E. Amplatz	(Austria)	15, 17, -16
J. Hansen	(Den.)	-18, -22

Mike Bush (0 - 5)

LOST

D. Welsman	(Wales)	20, -13, -13
N. Thomas	(Wales)	-10, -18
A. Griffiths	(Wales)	-18, -15
C. Pedersen	(Den.)	-17, -9
M. Daugard	(Den.)	-22, -20

After the disappointing relegation–what a terrible word–in 1979 in North Korea to the second division, we fought our way back and won the second division again in Novi Sad, Yugoslavia in 1981. Back to the elite division in Tokyo 1983. One of the hardest things is to keep everyone happy on a team of five. The fifth player wants to play but it can be a tough time when to play them. We decided to play Mike Bush against Wales–Mike lost all three and we were just two points from elimination.

In 1986 the USATT instituted a training program at the Lake Placid Olympic Center. I was the coach and we had seven Men and five Women that participated for the nine months. The Women players were Cheryl Dadian, Carole Davidson, Kim Gilbert, Vicky Wong, and Ardith Lonnon. The photo is as we head out on our three-mile run around the lake. The girls have started their run already.

L-R: Khoi Nguyen, Coach Dan, Khoa Nguyen, Brandon Olson, Perry Schwartzberg, Jerry Thrasher, Randy Seemiller, and Brian Masters.

Here's a photo with my Dad late in my career at the Indianapolis 4-star tourney. Dave Elwood was the promoter, and the event was held at the Indianapolis Convention Center in 1987.

Holding summer camps was so much fun back in the day. All the junior players stayed at our house. Here is one from the 70s, with Eric Boggan, Scott Boggan, Larry Thoman, and my three brothers, Rick, Randy, and Tim.

In the second photo, Dan Jr. (summer of 1992, about to turn two) is imitating Larry Hodges reading the newspaper. Larry taught Dan Jr. to say, "Two hundred and eighty-nine," though he had no idea what that meant. Then Larry would say, "Dan, what's 17 times 17?", and Dan would say, in his high-pitched voice, "Two hundred and eighty-nine!" and everyone would laugh and be impressed.

WINNING TABLE TENNIS

SKILLS, DRILLS, AND STRATEGIES

Dan Seemiller Mark Holowchak

My how to play "Winning Table Tennis" has been updated and is back on the market. The book is available at Amazon.com.

Coaching in South Bend for 23 years has been a great opportunity to keep me in the sport. Here's a few champs: Joey Cochran, Jared Lynch, and Dan Jr. at the annual Robo-Pong St. Joe Valley Open.

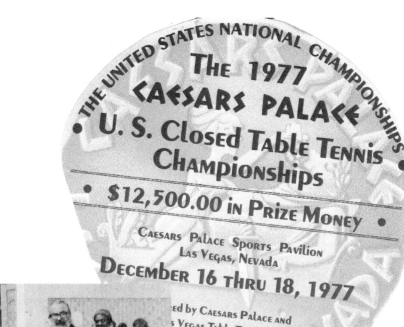

THE UNITED STATES NATIONAL CHAMPIONSHIPS

THE 1977 CAESARS PALACE

• U.S. Closed Table Tennis Championships

• $12,500.00 in Prize Money •

CAESARS PALACE SPORTS PAVILION
LAS VEGAS, NEVADA

DECEMBER 16 THRU 18, 1977

...ed by CAESARS PALACE and
...s VEGAS Table Tennis Association —
...ctioned by
...E UNITED STATES
...able Tennis Association

**Strikers at the 1976 U.S. Open.
Left: Charlie Wuvanich and me;
Above: Tim Boggan and Fuarnado
Roberts; Below: Mike Bush.
Photos by Houshang Bozorgzadeh**

1976 U.S. Open

So it's on to 1976, and what a newsmaker year this was going to be. The 1976 U.S. Open was held in Philadelphia. In 1976 I was the #1 player in the U.S. and money was hard to come by. Nearly 800 players entered. The prizes were very small. Dick Miles and Herb Vichnin were the organizers. Men's Singles had a $200 first prize, $100 second prize, and 50 dollars each for the semifinals. There were almost 800 players there. Just ridiculous.

In 1976 I made a tough decision to go on strike at the U.S. Open in Philadelphia. Many people were disappointed in not seeing me participate. It was embarrassing to carry a sign for four days. There was chaos and hard feelings. The police were summoned a couple of times. Sometimes you have to make a stand–if you want to be a professional, you can't play for nothing. The next Nationals at Las Vegas offered 10 times the prize money.

THE TABLE TENNIS REPORT

MONTHLY   JULY 1983

Danny Seemiller (U.S.A.)
American Champion in 1982.
Spectators' favorite at 37th
Tokyo Worlds.

My favorite shot is the forehand out of the backhand corner. The only problem is recovering back into position.

Tip: Win all three phases of the game: offense, defense, and serve/receive.

Butterfly Team (2)
U·S·A·
Swaythling Cup : No. 13
Corbillon Cup : No. 20

Alice Green

Men's Team successfully remains in the first category.

Eric Boggan

Ricky Seemiller

In 1983 our team defeated Russia 5-3 to finish 13th in Division 1. This was the highest finish for a U.S. Team in more than 60 years. Eric was unstoppable, winning 12 matches in a row and making the final 16 in singles. I won three versus Russia and almost defeated Cai Zhenhua. Rick defeated Appelgren and Orlowski. Scott and Attila had both won U.S. Singles titles. We had many good teams but this one was the best.
L-R: Attila, Dan, Eric, Scott, Rick and a happy Houshang.

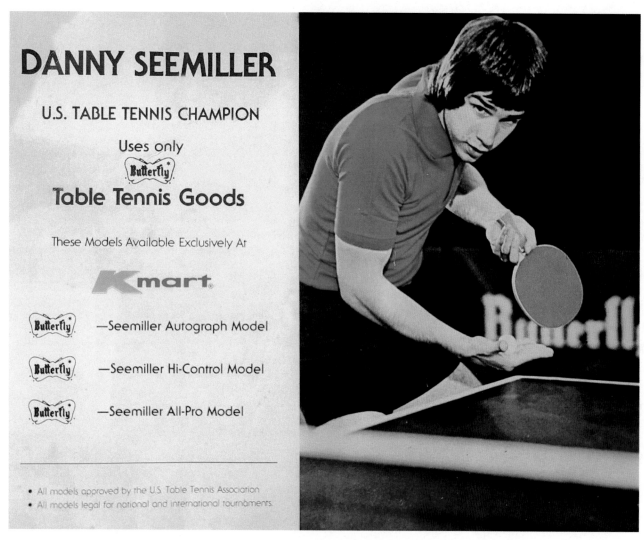
My first big break as a professional was in 1978. Kmart and Butterfly signed a five-year deal to sell my racket exclusively. There were 1,700 Kmart stores at the time and each one ordered 60 rackets. That's an initial order of 102,000. They ordered 20 each of the three different models– $7.99, $9.99, and 11.99. I used to love going into their stores and see them. The royalty checks kept me training hard and able to travel.

Tip: Underspin loop fundamentals:
1. Lower racket below table surface.
2. Use legs to lift and drive forward.
3. Change shoulder angle from square to angled.
4. Top of the bounce or just after.
5. The #1 goal here is to create quality spin.

Seemiller Stars in Table Tennis

Grand Rapids, Mich., May 30 (UPI)--The Japanese national table tennis team defeated an American all-star team yesterday, winning 8 of 11 matches, but it was Dan Seemiller who stole the show.

Seemiller, of Pittsburgh, accounted for all of the United States team's points by beating the three top-ranking Japanese players. The 19-year-old Seemiller defeated Nobuhiko Hasegawa, 21-6, 21-17, Tokio Tasaka, 21-9, 21-11, and Norio Takashima, 6-21, 21-17, 21-13.

(from the May 31 New York Times)

When I was 19 years old–1974–I was still conflicted about my decision to give up on a baseball career. This result gave me the feedback that TT was the right choice. The three Japanese players I won against that night were #2, #4, and #11 in the world rankings.

Coaching at the Sydney Olympics was so very memorable. The athlete's village was just across the way where most of the venues were. One could easily travel within 10 minutes to most of the sports. Every day free tickets were available for the U.S. contingent and the weather was perfect. For the 18-hour flight it was important that the middle seat was empty.

This was a culmination of hundreds of hours of training in the barn in our backyard and playing at South Park TTC in Pittsburgh. Rick, Randy, and I win the 1978 U.S. Open Teams in Detroit. Randy pulls the big upset as he defeats Eric Boggan in the 8th match to tie it and Rick defeats Scott Boggan to win the 9th 5-4.

Porch photo, L-R, front row: Randy, Tim. **Back**: Me, Rick

Tip: Know your distances and risk. Crosscourt is 10' 3", down the middle 9' 6", down the line 9'.

The most successful team I ever coached was the Pan Am one in 1999 in Winnipeg. Our team won the Gold and David Zhuang won gold in the singles. Only two medals available and we won two gold. This was my first big tourney as coach. In the final of the team versus Argentina we changed our order, as their #1 was very strong and our chances were better by switching our #1 to doubles. The order of play was a new one and somewhat confusing. I wrote the order down and checked several times to make sure I had the right one. Believe it or not, when the first match was called, they announced the wrong player and insisted they were right. I was shocked– could I have looked at this so long that I messed it up??? The umpire wanted to play but I needed to see the original lineup sheet, and this delayed the match. I was right, and somehow they had switched the order. I'll never forget the look on our players faces when they called David out instead of Eric. It was, "Coach, did you make a mistake?" No, I did not. *Whew!*
L-R: Dan, David Zhuang, Eric Owens, Todd Sweeris, and Bob Fox (Team Leader)
Photo by Aly Salam.

It's rare any day to gather the whole family together. My Dad's 88th birthday was the occasion, July 6, 2009.
Front: Tim, Dan, Ray Sr., Bill, Randy
Back: Ray, Cindy, Lynne, Jean, Rick
Inset: Mom–Dorothy

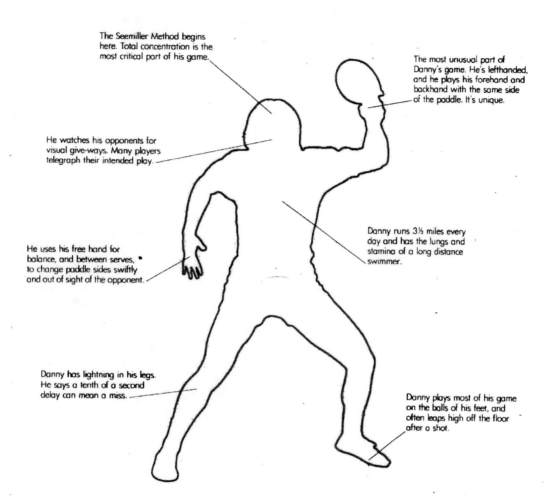

The Seemiller Method begins here. Total concentration is the most critical part of his game.

The most unusual part of Danny's game. He's lefthanded, and he plays his forehand and backhand with the same side of the paddle. It's unique.

He watches his opponents for visual give-ways. Many players telegraph their intended play.

Danny runs 3½ miles every day and has the lungs and stamina of a long distance swimmer.

He uses his free hand for balance, and between serves, to change paddle sides swiftly and out of sight of the opponent.

Danny has lightning in his legs. He says a tenth of a second delay can mean a miss.

Danny plays most of his game on the balls of his feet, and often leaps high off the floor after a shot.

He's the quiet American, the modest youngster from the hills of a steeltown, Pittsburgh, Pennsylvania, USA, who never picked up a paddle until he was twelve, who never learned to change his style from that of a beginner's, the kid who "didn't like to lose," and so he learned to win.

He's the most unorthodox player in the game, full of inconsistencies of style and table tennis ironies that baffle his opponents and amaze his spectators.

Leaping after shots, then "punching" the ball with a slam and a spin, floating the ball with the anti-top spin side of his paddle, exploding with his killing and crazy backhand—that's the Seemiller Method of table tennis.

It may be the method that soon places a table tennis ball in the American Eagle's nest.

Stellan Bengtsson, 1971 World Champion.
Sequence photo: Stellan loops a topspin drive down the line in the world final versus Itoh.

Tip: Photo 1: Total focus preparing to receive serve. The most difficult task to master in the sport.

51ST ROBO-PONG
ST. JOSEPH VALLEY OPEN

**SBTTC JUNIORS TEAM FROM LEFT:
MATT, MARTIN, COACH, DIONTA, DOMINIQUE AND DION**

Mark Hazinski
& Joe Cochran
Over 75 Years
of SBTTC's
dedication to
our Juniors!!

Here's a photo of some of South Bend TTC's junior team.

Going through the highs and lows of competing can be very disappointing. Here is a low point in my career. Just lost a close National Men's final to Attila Malek, 3-2, 21-18 in the fifth. Second year in a row to lose in the final. This was held at Caesar's Palace and ESPN filmed the final.

In North Korea with Dave Philip. We are about to go on a boat ride during our day off. We had wanted to cancel but our interpreter got all upset, saying we must go or else he would have trouble. The whole ride was a propaganda show but the weather was nice.

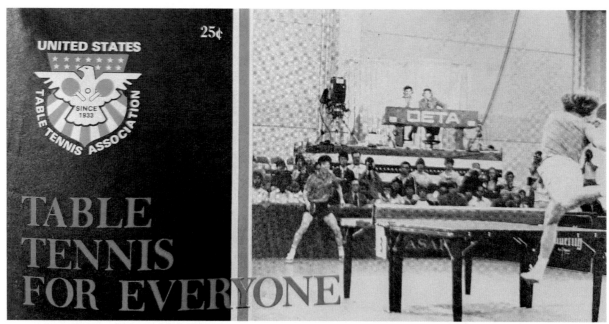

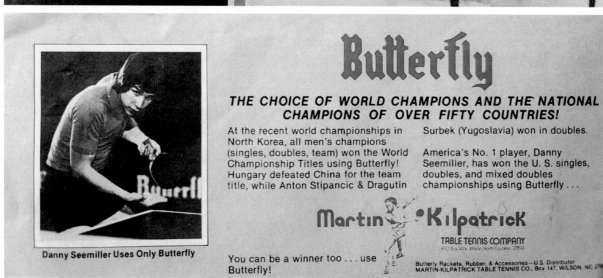

Here's a USTTA pamphlet from 1979, front and back cover.

Tip: The Backhand loop is a valuable weapon to have in one's arsenal. Keys are good balance, wrist action, and friction. The stroke is performed like throwing a frisbee.

DAN SEEMILLER

NATIONAL COACH OF THE YEAR

Dan Seemiller moved to South Bend in 1996 to coach at the 12-table South Bend Table Tennis Club. Practice is held five times a week with Varsity, Junior Varsity, and Cadet teams. He currently coaches the South Bend Junior Program. Dan's students include many of the best junior players in the U.S., with several achieving rankings in the top 10 for their age group. He currently coaches Mark Hazinski the top Under-16 Junior in the U.S. Seemiller's goal is to work with kids that are 11 to 15 years old and send them to international tournaments to see if possible stars can be developed from that group. He feels that if athletes know if they do well they will get more competition trips and become more serious about the sport. For the future, he believes in identifying more players at an earlier age.

Seemiller is the only player in the world with a grip named after him – the "Seemiller grip," which he developed and used throughout his career. At one point, players with this grip dominated table tennis in the U.S. with 80 percent of the U.S. team using it at one point. Eric Boggan, the highest ranked USA player of the past 25 years, learned most of the techniques of the grip from Seemiller who was the second highest ranked USA player of the past 25 years. The grip, in which a player uses the same side of the racket for both backhand and forehand, is one of the three main grips used in table tennis.

Seemiller's most recent accomplishments include coach of the Pan Am Team in 1999; gold medals were won in both the team and men's singles competition.

MASAAKI TAJIMA

DEVELOPMENTAL COACH OF THE YEAR

Masaaki Tajima started playing table tennis at San Francisco State University in 1970, while majoring in fine arts. He soon found a club, and by 1976, he was a 2200 level player. About that time, he was elected president of the club (San Francisco) and his priority changed from player to organizer. Although the club was the largest in Northern California with many kids playing, there were no coaches or programs. Tajima realized that to maintain or sustain growth, they needed a club coach with a coaching program. Since the association did not have a national coaching program at the time and coaches were hard to find, especially non-paid volunteer coaches, he decided to become a coach.

As a self-taught player studying tapes and going to virtually every tournament to learn, Tajima became an effective coach, and he believed that being a good player was secondary to being a good teacher. In 1979, he went to Japan to study coaching and took courses in sport psychology and human behavior.

In 1989, Tajima founded the Sunset Table Tennis Club in San Francisco primarily for developing junior players. When the nationals came to the University of California at Berkeley, it was a watershed event that changed the direction of his life. That year, two of his students won age events, his club was packed (still is) and the association asked him to start a coaches and schools program in his region.

By 1993, 16 coaches were recruited and certified and many of them have started their own coaching programs. Currently, Tajima has 24 adult and junior students.

Among Sunset Table Tennis Club's achievements are 12 National, U.S. Open and Junior Olympic titles. Some notable players who went through Tajima's program are Peter Zajac, Mark Liu, Shashine Shodhan, and Jackie Lee.

Tajima is a certified National Level coach.

In 2000 I was awarded the National Coach of the Year from the US Olympic Committee. In those days, the USOC awarded the top coaches with a trip to New York City and my daughter Sarah was able to go. We stayed at the Marriott in Times Square. This was early in January 2001, and one segment of the trip was to go up the World Trade Center at 8:45 in the morning, and we were on the top deck until 9:15 or so. If this were eight months later in September, it's hard to imagine as the 9/11 attack happened at 9 am. Masaaki Tajima also was on the trip as the Developmental Coach of the Year.

Love this facility, with the wood floor and the balcony above to watch the play. We have been using this IUSB facility for many years for our Robo-Pong St. Joe Valley Open. Thanks to Newgy, Visit South Bend, and Butterfly, our long-time sponsors.

The World Racquets Championship 1979. This was on CBS Sports and we had to play every sport but our own. I made the Tennis and Badminton finals. Playing Vilas in racquetball was a physical battle. I used all three of my timeouts as our rallies were long. After I called the third one at 18-all, Vilas, who is supremely fit from clay court tennis, gave me a look like, "Come on, you need another break?" CBS showed more of this match than any other on the program. Great exposure for TT.

L-R: 2nd from left Marty Hogan, Racquetball; Dan Seemiller, Table Tennis; Sharif Khan, Squash; Hilary Hilton, Platform Tennis; Rudy Hartono, Badminton; and Guillermo Vilas, Tennis.

第46回
西日本卓球選手権大会

開催期日　昭和58年2月19日〜20日
会　　場　柳　井　市　体　育　館
第二会場　柳井小学校体育館（ジュニア）

写真は45回大会の入賞者

準優勝 長谷川　男子単優勝 D.シーミラー　3位 A.ステパンチチ　3位 坂本

女子単優勝 安海淑

女子複優勝
安海淑(左)
黄男淑 組

男子複優勝 西村(左)・川村組

ジュニア
男子優勝
橋本

ジュニア
女子優勝
室井

主催　山口県卓球協会　　　後援　日本卓球協会・山口県教育委員会・柳井市
　　　柳井市教育委員会　　　　　柳井市体育協会・朝日新聞社・NHK山口放送局
主管　柳井市卓球協会　　　　　　日刊スポーツ・山口放送・テレビ山口

Many memories from the annual Western Japan Open in Yanai City. I played in this ten times.
This was in the home town of Butterfly founder Hikosuke Tamasu, who sponsored this tourney.
This one sold out at 1200 entrants. In the previous one I defeated Sakamoto–the current Japan
champion–in the semis and Hasegawa in the final, who beat Stipancic in the other semifinal.
L-R: Nobuhiko Hasegawa, Me, Anton Stipancic, Kenichi Sakamoto

Seemillers Head Back To Scene Of Their 'Crime'

By JIM O'BRIEN

The Seemiller brothers begin an international tour today that will eventually take them to Yugoslavia and the 36th World Table Tennis Championships.

Novi Sad is the site of the demanding 12-day tournament, and it is a long way from home in Carrick for Danny and Ricky Seemiller.

They have been there before. It is a city the Seemillers will not soon forget.

They had a harrowing experience there six years ago.

In telling their frightening tale of foreign intrigue, the Seemillers take turns — the way they do in doubles competition — and smash the story back and forth like a pingpong ball.

It sounds like a story Ken Follett might have written. For the Seemillers, the memories are vivid: Machine guns pointed at them by members of the Yugoslavian military ... angry German shepherd guard dogs charging at them ... riding in cramped police vans ... being jailed in a windowless cell ... interrogated under harsh lights and, much to their relief, released at last into the dark of a cold night, not sure if they could reach their hotel.

"At first, it seemed like it would be an interesting experience, but it wasn't much fun," declared Danny, who is 26 and has been the No. 1-ranked table tennis player in the U.S. the past eight years.

"There was a time there when I never thought I'd ever see the light of day again," remarked Ricky, who's 22 and ranked No. 3.

They combine their talents to form the country's best doubles team and that's where they have the best chance to win a world title in the tournament — conducted every two years — that will be held April 14-26. Until then, they will tour Japan to get their games in order for the international test.

Let's go back with the Seemillers to their 1975 visit to Novi Sad.

"I was the oldest at 20 and the captain of the U.S. team," recalled Danny. "So I was in charge. On the final Sunday of the tournament, there was a two-hour break before the finals. We were out of it, but we wanted to watch it — a Chinese against a Swede — so we could learn from what they were doing. We decided to go mountain-climbing into these nearby hills and take some pictures of the city from up there."

So he and his kid brother — Ricky was 16 then — and a young man from Detroit, Mike Veillette, who had the camera, went sight-seeing.

"When we reached the third crest," said Danny, "we came upon a large sign. We couldn't read it, but it looked official."

Interjected Ricky: "We knew we shouldn't go past there. The sign was in a clearing that was surrounded by all these neatly clipped Christmas trees. Just as we were turning to go back down the hill, a German shepherd came running out from the trees and started snarling at us. It was in a real rage."

"It looked," recalled Danny, "like it would tear our legs off."

Ricky started running down the hill, despite his brother's plea to stop. "Then a guy came out of the bushes with a machine gun pointed at me," said Ricky. "That's when I stopped."

The man was in a military uniform. The Seemillers suspected they had stumbled onto a military encampment, or maybe a missile site.

"He couldn't speak English," said Danny. "We had our badges on from the tournament and, at first, we felt there'd be no problem. Another guard came out. They held us there for an hour in the cold. Then a police van came up the side of the mountain; there was no road."

The three young men were frisked before being shoved into the small van, which was like a dog catcher's wagon.

"They went back down the mountain and didn't miss a bump along the way," said Ricky. "We were bouncing all over the place. We could see out a small peep hole and all the people were looking at us from the porches and doorways of the film developed to see what pictures they had taken.

Then they were called, one at a time, into an interrogation room. Each of them sat on a stool, with harsh lights directly in their eyes, and asked about 10 questions. A woman stenographer sat in the background, taking down their testimony. "It was just like in the movies, like 'Midnight Express' or something," said Ricky. And it was for real.

When they were finally told they were free to go, the boys learned that they were 10 miles from the hotel where the contestants were being housed. It was 1:30 a.m. when they were released. They were also their homes. They seemed ve afraid of the police. As we passe they'd disappear into their home

"Once we got into the van," Ric continued, "I started to get scared started to think, 'Hey, they could k us.' Who'd investigate? Only one g from Canada knew that we we anywhere. The first thing that can to my mind was, 'Who knew? Whe would they start looking for us?'"

The three young men were he for 14 hours. They were kept in wooden cell that had no window "You couldn't look out, or get out said Danny. "There were just fo walls."

The camera was confiscated an told that a bus would come by. Th weren't told when. "We asked they could take us back to t hotel," said Danny.

That's when a guard, who h been acting all day as if he did understand a word they were sa ing, snapped, "What do you thi we're running here — a t service?"

The Seemillers can smile abo the story now, but when quizz about their plans on this trip to No Sad, they both agreed they wou not do any mountain-climbing sightseeing this time around. Th will stay close to the table tenr action.

Playing on the U.S. National team from 1973-1985, my brother and I traveled all over the world. In 1975 we were in Yugoslavia, a Communist country at the time, and we got in some trouble. Article is from the *Pittsburgh Press*, Feb. 8, 1981.

Winning the CNE tourney was a thrill. Zlatko Cordas from Yugoslavia and I had a close match and friendly battle, from the look of the post-match handshake. Zlatko played on the great Yugoslavian teams with Surbek and Stipancic, and later had success coaching the German Men's National Team. Photo has the ball, racket, table, net, players, umpire, and spectators all in it.

The old USTTA patch that was popular on shirts back in the 70s.

Medals from the World Veterans in Las Vegas, Winnipeg, Rio de Janeiro, Dortmund, Athens, and Las Vegas Nationals in the middle.

Photo by Ellie Bozorgzad

The Nissen Open in Cedar Rapids, Iowa was an annual event run by my long-time coach Houshang. It was a 14-hour drive from Pittsburgh, but worth it every time to support him. The Nissen table was slow and fit my game. Made that long drive home Sunday night/Monday morning not so bad.

L-R: U.S Team Captain Houshang Bozorgzadeh, Nissen Open Tournament Director; 3rd Place finisher Rey Domingo, Winner Danny Seemiller, holding the John Stillions Memorial Trophy; Runner-up Scott Boggan; 4th Place finisher Brandon Olson; and Tournament Sponsor George Nissen.

VOL. 44, No. 4, NOV.-DEC. 1976

Table Tennis

THE OFFICIAL MAGAZINE OF THE UNITED STATES TABLE TENNIS ASSOCIATION

Tim Boggan, Editor
12 Lake Avenue, Merrick, N.Y. 11566
Published bi-monthly
Second Class Matter, Post Office, Massapequa, N.Y. 11758

USOTC MEN'S TEAM WINNERS: (left to right) JOE ROKOP, MVP AWARD WINNER, DANNY SEEMILLER, RICKY SEE-MILLER, AND LARRY GOLDFARB.

USOTC WOMEN'S TEAM WINNERS: (left to right) NPC D-J LEE, HE-JA LEE, MVP AWARD WINNER IN SOOK BHUSHAN, AND NANCY NEWGARDEN.

JUNIOR TEAM WINNERS: (left to right) MVP AWARD WINNER SCOTT BOGGAN, MIKE LARDON, AND ERIC BOGGAN.

Photos by Neal Fox

Playing in the National team tourney was on our schedule every year over the Thanksgiving weekend in Detroit. So many matches and the whole TT community and the Canadians were always there. No better feeling than sharing a victory with teammates. Rick and my name are switched in top-left photo–I am third from the left. From 1976!

Benson & Hedges
"Love Bird"
TABLE TENNIS
TOURNAMENT

NATIONAL ARENA - JUNE 4,5,6

Playing at the Jamaican Open in Kingston at the National Arena was an experience like no other. The Jamaicans are very vocal and the energy in their Arena was second to none. There were several thousand spectators in attendance each night.

Family photo from the 50s. Starting from the right: Aunt Lois, Ray Jr., Me being held by Aunt Alice, Bill, My Dad Ray, Jeanne, Mom Dorothy, Aunt Molly, Uncle Ted, Uncle Al, Aunt Betty, not sure of the last couple.

USTTA-ESPN Announce One-Year TV Contract

52 ninety-minute table tennis shows to be aired

Back in 1980 ESPN needed programming to fill their 24-hour sports program. 52 shows at TT tourneys around the country. ESPN hired mostly local crews and of course they had never done TT before. The Eastern Open in Pittsburgh was promoted heavily by the college and 750 spectators were there to watch. Just before the semifinals an electric fire caused by overloading the circuits sent acrid, thick black smoke into the hall and everyone had to hurry out of the building. No one was hurt and the tourney continued two hours later, with most of the audience gone. Another time in North Carolina we played the finals at 1 a.m. as the crew had problems.

1986
11th ANNUAL NISSEN OPEN
TABLE TENNIS CHAMPIONSHIPS
and
UNITED STATES WORLD TEAM TRIALS

How It Feels To Be Number 1
DANNY SEEMILLER
Nine Times Nissen Singles Champion

October 4, 5, 6, 7, 1986
UNIVERSITY OF NORTHERN IOWA WEST GYMNASIUM
CEDAR FALLS, IOWA

The Nissen Open was held annually in Cedar Rapids, Iowa. A long drive from Pittsburgh–14 hours. Our U.S. Team Coach Houshang was the organizer and Nissen Company supplied the prize money. Nissen was prominent in schools across the country with their trampolines, TT tables, and exercise equipment. The Nissen table was slow–very durable and made for school use. "Here is the program from the 1986 Nissen that you autographed for me. I was about 14 years old. It was a big thrill, truly. thank you. Have a good day." ~Aaron

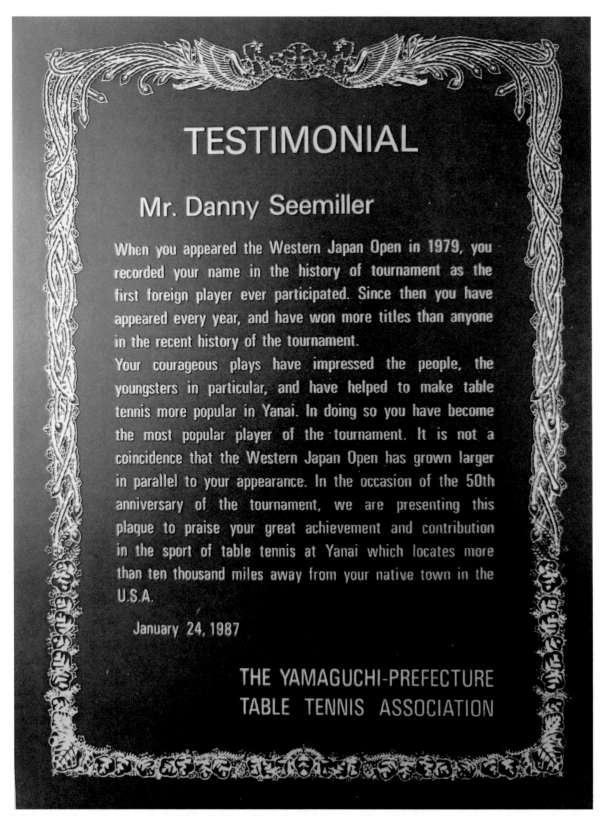

TESTIMONIAL

Mr. Danny Seemiller

When you appeared the Western Japan Open in 1979, you recorded your name in the history of tournament as the first foreign player ever participated. Since then you have appeared every year, and have won more titles than anyone in the recent history of the tournament.

Your courageous plays have impressed the people, the youngsters in particular, and have helped to make table tennis more popular in Yanai. In doing so you have become the most popular player of the tournament. It is not a coincidence that the Western Japan Open has grown larger in parallel to your appearance. In the occasion of the 50th anniversary of the tournament, we are presenting this plaque to praise your great achievement and contribution in the sport of table tennis at Yanai which locates more than ten thousand miles away from your native town in the U.S.A.

January 24, 1987

THE YAMAGUCHI-PREFECTURE TABLE TENNIS ASSOCIATION

This is my favorite trophy. When I first signed with Butterfly of Japan, they promised to bring me over each year for a month to train and play in this tourney–the Western Japan Open. There were 1200 players attending. I won the tournament five times and finished second four times.

48

STELLAN BENGTSSON
World's Singles Champion

KJELL JOHANSSON

ISTVAN JONYER

In the table tennis world of the early 70's these players were the ones I looked up to and learned from. Stellan Bengtsson of Sweden, 1971 World Singles Champion, world doubles champ, and ranked #1 in the world. Kjell Johansson of Sweden, his nickname was the "Hammer," the best forehand of that era. World team and world doubles champ with Stellan. Istvan Jonyer of Hungary, 1975 world singles champ–strong topspin game with great touch.

E PUPIL. Danny Seemiller of Pittsburgh awaits the service of his teacher, [...]ris of Grand Rapids, Mich., in the championship match of the Gateway Open tal[...] tournament yesterday at Edwardsville. Seemiller won, three games to two. (Po[...] Photo by Ken J. MacSwan)

Training in Grand Rapids with Dell Sweeris, we traversed all over the Midwest playing almost every weekend somewhere. Dell had a Dodge Rambler, and we pulled a trailer with equipment for sale. It was fun and always challenging. Having a tourney to look forward to made the training during the week more energized and purposeful. Here Dell's giving me the Tomahawk or tennis serve so popular back then.

DOUBLES EXCITEMENT - GERMANS, AFTER GETTING EDGE BALL, GO ON TO BEAT AMERICANS.
DEUCE IN THE 5TH

1977 U.S. Open doubles final in Los Angeles. My partner, on left, is Ray Guillen. The German pair, Leiss and Stellwag, just lobbed an edge ball to gain the ad, 21-20. You can see the Germans feel fortunate and we are very disappointed. We lose this one, 22-20.

Here's my father cooking dinner for the TT summer camp members who stayed at the house. My Dad loved to cook. It was chaotic but fun with eight or more staying at our home. TT all day and softball, mini golf, or wiffleball at night. That's my sister Cindy hiding behind the fork–it's time for cake–and Eric Boggan on the left. And to think a few years later it's Eric beating me in the U.S. final in 1978.

It was declared "Table Tennis Day" in Pittsburgh, February 23,1989. Our club worked closely with the Parks and Recreation Dept. and the Commissioners of Allegheny County to secure club space. Our club guys who volunteered their time: Back row is Bob Doby, Club Secretary; 3rd is Stan Carrington, President, and 5th is Barry Rodgers, Treasurer.

This is the best shot I ever made. Second round of the worlds in 1983 Tokyo versus world #2 Cai Zhenhua of China. We were both lefties and he hooked a ball to my left that I couldn't reach without diving. I curved this shot in the left corner and won the point. Score was 16-13 for me at the time, down 2-1 in games. I then ran out the game 21-13.

Photo 1: Here Shigeo Itoh, 1969 world champion, shows you why he was called Superman in his prime. What an amazing shot.

Photo 2: Cheng Min-Chih pivots around the BH corner for a FH crosscourt.

Tip: The forehand attack from the backhand corner is a very important technique in the sport. Why does it work?
1. You have more time to execute the stroke.
2. The table doesn't impede your movement forward.

My book "Winning Table Tennis" was distributed by Human Kinetics in several countries. Here's a copy in Korean. It is also available at <u>Amazon.com</u> in English.

Photo Copyright 1979 by Neal Fox

U.S. – NORTH KOREA MEN'S TEAM MATCH AT PYONGYANG WORLD'S
DANNY LOSES TO HONG CHOL . . . U.S. TEAM LOSES 5-0

It's 1979 and our team has to play the North Korean team in Pyongyang. This is the World Championships and there are 22,000 fans rooting for their countryman. My match was 18-all in the final game when I won the point. There was no cheering immediately after, but then a big roar as the North Korean umpire gave my opponent the point. I refused to play for about five minutes, but it became too hostile and dangerous, so I had to play on and lost.

Yanai, Japan

Danny Seemiller Wins Third Western Japan Open

by Dick Yamaoka

The 1984 Western Japan Open was held at the City Gymnasium of Yanai, Japan, February 18-19. Over 1,600 entrants participated in the two day tournament!

Yanai, a small city of 30,000, is obviously a table tennis town. The city's Mayor, Mr. Shiraji, was the honorary Tournament Director and he was in the hall throughout the competition. However, the real reason table tennis is so popular in Yanai is because it is the birthplace of Mr. Hikosuke Tamasu, President of the Tamasu Company of Tokyo (Butterfly).

It was the 47th Western Japan Open and Mr. Tamasu has participated in all of them as either a player or as an official. It was Mr. Tamasu's decision to invite Danny Seemiller to the tournament five years ago to give a boost to the competition. Since then the tournament has grown steadily and considerably. This year there were entries from four foreign countries. Besides the USA, players came from Brazil, Korea, and Chinese Taipei, a new member of the ITTF.

This year, the Western Japan Open received considerable amount of attention. It was the very first tournament held in Japan in which the new two color racket rule and new service rules were enforced. It was also the first tournament that the Chinese Taipei team par-

Danny Seemiller, again the winner in Japan

ticipated in Japan since becoming an ITTF member. Newspapers gave good coverage producing excellent publicity for the event.

A press conference for the foreign players was held the day before competition but we arrived two days before. A small town nearby wanted Danny Seemiller to visit so we went there first. There were 40 children between 7-12 years-old and by their request, a coaching clinic was held. Danny played with each of them and he quickly became their hero. They all got his autograph

and I could feel the excitement among them. They said that they wanted him to win the tournament and Danny commented to me: "You know, I just can't let them down. I have to win." I think their support definitely helped him.

In order to play so many matches, all of them had to be the best of three. All doubles were played the first day. Danny's partner was former World Champion Hasegawa and they breezed through to the final.

See Japan page 6

Playing and training in Japan was so important for my career. The sport is taken seriously there. Elementary schools, high schools, and colleges all use TT in physical education and have teams that compete. The Western Japan Open would be the end of each visit. My record with the Asian players was always strong. I had more trouble with the Europeans and their close to the net game.

58

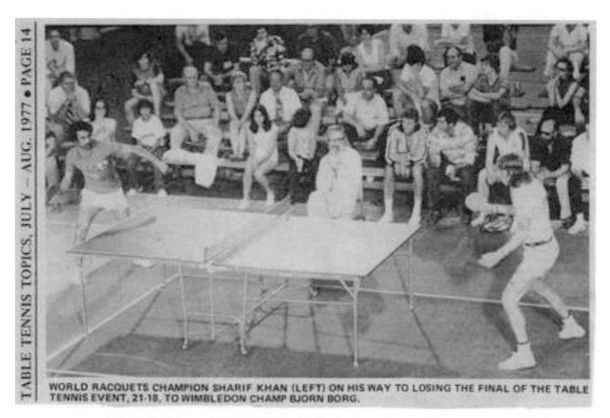

WORLD RACQUETS CHAMPION SHARIF KHAN (LEFT) ON HIS WAY TO LOSING THE FINAL OF THE TABLE TENNIS EVENT, 21-18, TO WIMBLEDON CHAMP BJORN BORG.

CBS hosted the World Racquets Championships for three years, 1977-1979. Tim Boggan is the umpire. (He turned 90 on Sept. 25, 2020.) Tim was the President of USTTA. My Dad and Scott Boggan are in the third row, arms crossed. I participated all three years. Tennis, badminton, squash, racquetball, and table tennis. We each played all the sports except our own.

Photo 1: Kohji Kimura launches a forehand.
Photo 2: Dragutin Surbek spins a heavy one.

Tip: Power is a major force in all sports. In table tennis this relates to the speed and spin on your drives. Using the whole body when attacking can make it impossible to defend.

New Champion. Danny Seemiller (U.S.A)

▲全米選手権では伏兵ボーガンに敗れ、来日後の試合でも長谷川に２連敗するなど気落ちしていたシーミラー（アメリカ）だったが、１戦１戦を集中して戦うことで調子をあげ、準決勝、決勝では会心のプレーをみせて２度目の優勝を飾った

My backhand serve was a big weapon. It was hard to read and you can see by my action I'm not just putting it into play. The key is to pull the elbow across and back in a semi-circle and fast.

Tip: Develop quality serves and be unique whenever possible–racket speed is essential. Use the body to create momentum. The Backhand sidespin serve is very useful and is making a comeback in today's game.

DAN SEEMILLER, 19-year-old table tennis pro, competes at 1974 table tennis tournament at the University of Pennsylvania.

Playing table tennis took me from local tourneys, to state tourneys like this one at the University of Pennsylvania, to competing at the sport in more than 50 countries. My five favorite countries: Japan, Sweden, England, Canada, and Germany.

Tip: Use your free arm to help create balance and power.

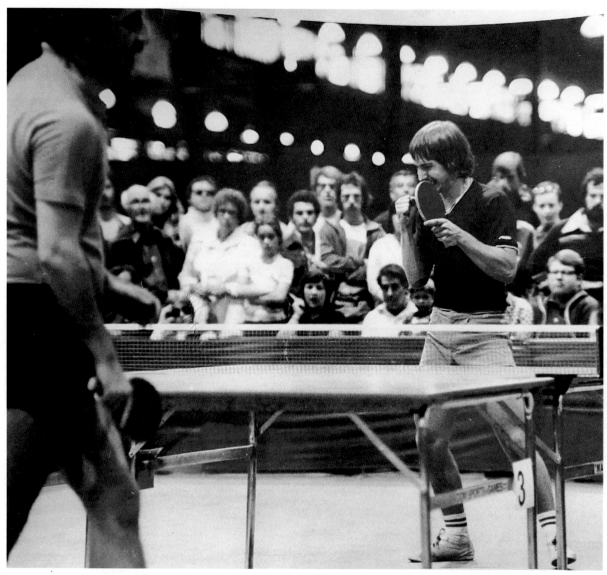

Moment of victory in the Canadian Open against Zlatko Cordas from Yugoslavia. This was an extremely hard final. The CNE tourney in Toronto was held every Labor Day weekend in September and signaled the beginning of a new season.

Tip: To make comebacks takes never giving up and not focusing on the score. Nothing more satisfying in sports than turning what could be a loss into a win.

Our U.S. Men's Team in Toronto at the Canadian National Exhibition as we ready to play the Canadian team in 1977. L-R: Rick Seemiller, Dean Galardi and Ray Guillen from California, me, and coach Houshang Bozorgzadeh from Iowa.

Tip: When you lose focus, which everyone does at some point, the key is to recognize it and recover as quickly as possible. Think of strategy and get your mind active again.

Working as a TV commentator is a challenge. Especially when you are going live. The heart starts to pound when the producer says 5, 4, 3, 2, 1....

Tip: When blocking one first needs to assess the quality of the attack for their response. If there is plenty of energy there, just redirect it. If it lands short or is weak, then block aggressively or counterattack.

Playing on the U.S. Team for several years, both Rick and I participated in many tourneys, like this one in Hong Kong in 1979.

Tip: Always go for the shot. Many times scrambling to win a point can make all the difference.

A veteran player at 23, the left-handed Seemiller defeated 37-year-old Dal Joon Lee to win the title.

Backed away from the table, Lee was almost helpless. The best he could manage was some high-trajectory lobs, which were usually pounded for winners. Seemiller won handily, 21–12, 21–10, 21–13. Still, in a sport where great players often peak at 18 or 19 and are burned out at 35, it was a credit to Lee that he was able to fight his way to the final.

With age such an important factor in table tennis, experts at the Closed—where on 42 tables nearly 465 players competed in 31 events ranging from veterans over 70 to boys under 11—spent a good deal of time analyzing the styles of promising juniors, kids who will soon be catching Seemiller, who at 23 is losing some juice. Already there are several who play with his palm-first basement style, among them his two brothers, Ricky, 19, and Randy, 17, and 14-year-old Eric Boggan, who four weeks before the Closed upset Seemiller in a match at the National Team championships in Detroit. None of these did anything spectacular at the Closed, but Mike Bush, 21, and Rutledge Barry, 15, reached the men's semis, the farthest either had ever gone in so strong a tournament.

The most promising youngster of all was a pale, slender 10-year-old named Sean O'Neill from Vienna, Va., who took the Boys Under 11 event. His game is still in the formative stages, but he has fundamentally sound strokes and plays with passion. His mother Kathy says, "My husband and I have already decided that Sean will be a full-time player. He's playing at least three hours a day, and it's what he loves best. There'll be money in this sport in a few years, and Sean, we think, is in the right place at the right time. The only problem is expenses. We're already spending about $10,000 a year taking him to tournaments. To save money, only one of us goes along now. Pat took him to England for the Worlds; I got Las Vegas."

Sean, a 4′ 7″ 68-pounder with blond hair and blue eyes, already has clear notions about the kind of player he wants to be. "I don't like the Chinese style," he says. "They're too much like machines, too mechanical. My favorite player is Jonyer." Istvan Jonyer, of Hungary, won the world singles title in 1975.

Unfortunately, Sean's lack of respect for the Chinese classicists has been the prevailing attitude among U.S. juniors and their coaches for some time, and it has probably kept them from reaching the world-class levels that American players attained from the '30s through the '50s. As an embarrassing reminder that technique is all-important, two Korean women, both resident aliens, reached the finals of the women's singles at Las Vegas: In Sook Bhushan, a classic chopper, beat He-Ja Lee, Dal Joon's wife and a classic attacker, 3–0.

A native American nearly prevailed in the hard-rubber competition—the bow-and-arrow event, some call it, because hard-rubber rackets are so out of date; 47-year-old Marty Reisman (SI, Nov. 21) got to the final, only to lose to Franz-Joseph Hürmann, 28, of Phoenix, 3–1.

Finally, there was Chuck Burns of Detroit, a star in the 1940s, who as he headed toward one of the tables was asked which event he was about to play. "The only one I'm left in," said Burns, "the Senior Esquire Singles. It's the last one before the wooden box. I had to convince my opponent we should play it today. One of us might not be here tomorrow."

After the trophies were awarded, some of "tomorrow's" players were seen peering avidly down at the action in the Caesars Palace casino. These were the underage juniors, barred from the floor by Caesars' polite but firm security personnel. But today's player, Dan Seemiller, plunked some chips on the pass line, chose his dice and rolled them—palm first—onto the green cloth. A seven came up. It was a natural. **END**

A future star is 10-year-old Sean O'Neill, who impressed experts as he won the Boys Under 11 title.

Winning the 1977 U.S. Men's Nationals and then having it reported in *Sports Illustrated* made for a thrilling time.

Tip: Be aggressive when serving. Have two or three patterns that you use over and over again to increase your ability to anticipate the return. When receiving: Read the spin and depth, know your options, and be decisive.

67

Our South Bend club was blessed to have as a member Virgil Miller. Virgil was CEO of Newmar RV company and a lover of table tennis. When I first came to SB many years ago Virgil was instrumental in helping the club to keep me here when finances were thin. Virgil is seen here awarding the $5,000 first-place check to Ilija Lupulesku for winning the St. Joseph Valley Open. Newmar RV and Virgil Miller sponsored the prize money of $20,000.

Tip: When competing don't worry about winning and losing. That's not going to help. Just be prepared to perform, concentrate, and do your best. Take each point as if a match unto itself.

Dell Sweeris, multiple times national doubles champion, was my coach and mentor for several years in the 1970s. I moved to his hometown of Grand Rapids, Michigan, and we became daily practice partners. Dell's wife Connie won the U.S. Women's Singles championship in Atlanta in 1971.

U.S. AND NORTH KOREAN MEN'S TEAM, PYONGYANG, 1979

Our match with North Korea in 1979 was like no other, with 22,000 spectators cheering wildly for their team. It literally brought the house down. L-R: Dave Philip, myself, Rick Seemiller, Roger Sverdlik, Coach Houshang, and Scott Boggan in front.

70

Every year from 1979-1988 I visited Japan to participate in the Western Japan Open. I also stayed a few weeks to take advantage of the high-level training there. I was defending champion and I won the title five times. Here's the program cover for the tournament.

Tip: When looking at this program from the Western Japan Open it is clear the use of the free arm is essential to create balance and racket speed. How well do you use your free arm?

Photo by Ellie Bozorgzadeh

Nissen Open Champ Danny Seemiler, down 2-0 to Rey Domingo in 4-man round robin final, wins in 5.

1982 Nissen Open in Cedar Rapids, Iowa. Rey Domingo from New York was my opponent. He shows his frustration after leading most of the way. His paddle seems to be suspended in mid-air.

Tip: It's never over no matter how big the lead.

Ping-Pyongyang: Our table tennis brothers head for North Korea

By John Clemans

It began as a game British officers in India played to while away the long hours of boredom. A champagne cork, a dining room table and a slightly bemused attitude sufficed. Now the sport is played by ambitious professionals, the best of whom can smash the ball at speeds of 100 miles per hour. Players guard their favorite paddles like national secrets, and international competition is fierce. Ping-Pong—the game of 35 million Americans (only 29 million play tennis)—has come a long way.

On April 25, the United States Table Tennis Team will step even closer to the limelight when it becomes the first U.S. team ever to enter North Korea. In what promises to be the latest round of "Ping-Pong diplomacy" since the United States and China exchanged players in 1971, the U.S. team will play in the 35th World Table Tennis Championships in Pyongyang. Led by America's number-one player, Danny Seemiller, 24, the team will compete in the elite 16-nation first division for the first time in 30 years. Seemiller hopes that the North Korea trip will lift

Ping-Pong out of the basement where it has long languished as a favorite family pastime and into the spotlight where it belongs. "I'll bet I have 10,000 fans in Japan, but no one knows me here," laments Danny.

The roster of the U.S. men's team reads like a game of Ping-Pong: Danny Seemiller, Eric Boggan, Ricky Seemiller, Scott Boggan. For the Seemillers of Pittsburgh and the Boggans of Merrick, N.Y., table tennis is in the blood. Danny and Ricky, 21, are only two of five Ping-Ponging brothers. Eric, 15, and Scott, 17, were taught to play by

In the backyard chicken coop (below) at their Pittsburgh home, Danny Seemiller, 24 (at left), and his brother Ricky, 21, train table tennis hopefuls.

Ricky Seemiller leaps for a shot (above), demonstrating some of the muscle needed for pro table tennis.

The U.S. men's team (left) from left: Roger Sverdlik, Ricky and Danny Seemiller, Eric and Scott Boggan.

Ricky Seemiller goes for a smash (right), but has never beaten brother Danny, the number one U.S. player. They'll try for the world championship in late April.

their father, Tim Boggan, who once ranked seventh in this country. Not to be outdone, Roger Sverdlik, the final member of the men's team, has a brother who is the West Virginia champion. Table tennis just seems to run in the family.

At the head of the table is Danny, who has dominated U.S. table tennis since 1972. But only recently has he begun to net some returns on the game. "If I'm lucky, I could make $50,000 this year, less expenses," he predicts. A slice of that will come from clinics that he and Ricky host at their Pittsburgh training site—a converted chicken coop in the backyard. It was there that 10th-grader Eric Boggan, the John McEnroe of table tennis (a reputation he earned because of his petulant table manners), perfected the unorthodox "Seemiller grip," which he used to upset Danny last December in the U.S. Closed. (The grip, America's secret weapon when they visit Pyongyang, allows the player to hit both backhand and forehand shots with the same side of the paddle.) "We taught the kid to play, and now he beats us," fumes Ricky.

But a more brotherly bunch of adversaries would be hard to find. "We're actually more like one family than two," says Danny. "We all hang out together at tournaments, and the Boggans stay at our house for weeks on end." The Boggans are not the only players to frequent the chicken coop. As many as 28 table tennis hopefuls have been under the Seemiller roof at one time. Laughs Ricky, "It seems like we've trained the whole country."

The Seemillers practice four hours a day on their shots—the forehand loop, the lob, the drop shot and the smash. Danny, an all-around athlete who turned down a tryout with the Pittsburgh Pirates in 1972 to devote himself to table tennis, has the fastest smash in the world (clocked at more than 100 m.p.h.).

The U.S. team will travel to China after the championships for a series of exhibitions; players hope China will accept an invitation to the U.S. Open in June at Long Island's Nassau Coliseum. More than a thousand players from around the world will compete, making it the largest U.S. tournament in the sport's history.

On the verge of national recognition, Danny Seemiller hopes the North Korea trip will enable him to cash in on his superstar status. But if fame doesn't come his way, the trip won't have been a total loss. At the very least, America's number-one player will have perfected the delicate art of autographing Ping-Pong balls. □

Here is an article from US magazine from May, 1979. A very memorable and interesting time in North Korea, a country not seen by many. Things I remember most from the trip:

- How beautiful the landscape was.
- How clean the streets and subway system were.
- Being alarmed when upon arrival our passports were taken and were to be given back when we left.
- Listening to the leader Kim Il-Sung song all day everywhere.
- Everyone wearing the same clothes. Not many smiling faces.
- Tension from the authorities about us being there.
- Feeling great when our plane took off to head back home.

Photo copyright 1979 by Neal Fox

DANNY SEEMILLER:
PLAYING IN THE GERMAN BUNDESLEAGUE

Photo by David R. Moore

1977 U.S. OPEN TRIPLE CROWN WINNER
JOCHEN LEISS OF GERMANY

In 1977 I lost in the U.S. Open final to Jochen Leiss from Germany. Afterwards he invited me to play for his team in the Bundesliga. This is the top pro league, and the competition and training was high level and worth all the extra travel. I went back and forth to Europe eight times that year. Simex-Julich was the team name.

Tip: Every time you lose a match it is an opportunity to learn.

Moved to South Bend in 1996. Here is my first junior team. Thanks to Victor Tolkachev for coaching these youngsters before me as their fundamentals were excellent.
Check out our website at southbendtabletennis.com.

EARNING A SPOT AT THE TOP

U.S. champion Danny Seemiller won all 26 matches he played in the team event, but he still wasn't always happy with the way things were going . . .

Ricky Seemiller (above), Ray Guillen (below), and Dean Galardi all provided key victories for the U.S.A. men's team.

. . . Danny was happy with beating China's Kuo Yao Hua and Liao Fu-Min

In 1977 our U.S. Men's Team won the second division at the Birmingham, England World Championships. Our goal of competing in the top division was accomplished and each player did their part. We were now in with the elites–China, Korea, Japan, Sweden, and Germany.

Big match versus Hanno Deutz of Dusseldorf. Lots of energy as this was for first place in the German Bundesliga. Great crowd.

Tip: Ball placement is critical in table tennis. Attack the middle, the switch point between the forehand and backhand, and go wide when possible.

VOL. 42, NO. 4   NOVEMBER — DECEMBER 1974

Table Tennis

THE OFFICIAL MAGAZINE OF THE UNITED STATES TABLE TENNIS ASSOCIATION

T.   oggan, Editor
A   Merrick, N.Y. 11566
bi-monthly
Second Class Ma   ffice, Massapequa, N.Y. 11758

$1.00

At Jamaica:

U.S.A. BEATS ★ ★ ENGLAND, 3-2

THE WINNERS AND THEIR BOOTY. The victorious Americans hold their trophy aloft as cheers of congratulation echo round the Kingston Arena. From left: GEORGE BRATHWAITE, ANGELITA ROSAL, and TIM BOGGAN, President of the USA's table tennis association, with the Benson and Hedges Trophy. At right, BRATHWAITE, the hero of the tournament, who won the deciding game just in time, is hugged by his jubilant teammates, DANNY SEEMILLER and ROSAL. Braithwaite edged England's Ian Horsham 21-23, 21-14, 21-19, to carry the USA to a 3-2 victory.

— Jamaica Daily News photos by Roy Shakes

Our good friend and Hall-of-Famer George Braithwaite winning the key match. Here he is leading our U.S. team to victory over England. This event was played at the National gymnasium in Kingston, Jamaica.

79

Great memories from Sydney as coach of the USA Men's Team.

My dad was an Army Veteran who served in the Korean War. On November 12, 2009, my father Ray passed away. He was a caring family man who held two jobs most of his life to provide for the nine Seemiller children. My mother was a nurse and dad drove a bread truck. He never wanted any material things only to see that his children were taken care of. Dad was a doting husband to my mother Dorothy after her stroke–each and every day dedicated to taken care of her. This was taken at my high school Hall of Fame dinner.

A poster from the 1978 US Open in Oklahoma City. Really well run and the community provided big support. Several finals were on national TV on PBS.

USA Table Tennis Team
Games of the XXVIII Olympiad
Athens, Greece

When I moved my family in 1996 to South Bend, Indiana to become the coach of the SBTTC, Mark Hazinski was 10. Eight years later Mark made the Olympic Team, and I am named the coach for the Athens Games. Mark paired up with Ilija Lupulesku and they did well, reaching the third round before losing a very close one to a team from Taiwan. What else I remember about Athens was the daytime heat. Stay out of the sun from 12-5 pm. Traffic was brutal going to and from the venue. Ryu Seung-Min basking in his gold medal upset win at the Olympic Village. Sightseeing at the Acropolis and Parthenon. Walking through the town at night–cobblestone streets and small shops everywhere. One time I left my ID at the eating area and went out to the bus. Getting back in the village would be a problem. Luckily, Doru, our Women's coach, picked it up and saved me. He let me panic for a couple minutes first, though.

1975 World Champion Istvan Jonyer in singles performs his powerful forehand loop. He was also a power in doubles play, winning the world title two times. He also led Hungary to victory over China at the 1979 world teams. Second photo–a young Istvan competes against Chuang Tse-Tung, 3x world singles champ, at the 1971 worlds.

A trip that just didn't work out. Rick and I started off with a clinic in Kansas City. Taught for three days and were paid a little in cash and a check that bounced. On to Salt Lake City and we had car trouble and missed one day of a three-day mall exhibition. Then it was on to Phoenix for a major tourney and a rematch with a new rival from Thailand who had beaten me once already, Charlie Wuvanich. He had this serve and smash game that I had serious trouble handling. I led 19-16 in the final game, and with Charlie serving, he wins all five. Outrageous tough loss. Now we have to drive back to Pittsburgh. We are in my Chevy Vega and the engine blows just outside of Albuquerque. Here's my match with Charlie at the Nissen Open.
Photo by Gary Elwell

Having dinner in Tokyo with Shigeo Itoh and Nobuhiko Hasegawa. Nobuhiko on the right won the world singles title in 1967 and Shigeo Itoh won the 1969 championship. Etsuko was the interpreter. These two champions were my practice partners and mentors while in Japan for a month each year from 1979-1988. I can remember as a youngster in 1969 wondering what it would be like to play the world champion Itoh, and now I'm learning from him. It was surely an honor to tour with these two gentlemen and thanks to Butterfly for making it an annual trip.

At the 1989 U.S. Open in Ft. Lauderdale J-O Waldner needed a doubles partner. Mikael Appelgren hurt his shoulder the week before and withdrew. I was available and J-O ok'd the pairing. Jan-Ove was the world #1 so if we lose.... I was really nervous about accepting because my practice in the summer suffered because of the camps we ran in Pittsburgh. I almost said no because I knew my form wasn't the best, but how could I pass up the chance to play with possibly the greatest player ever to hold a racket? We had fun–lost in the semifinals 2-1, real close to a Korean pair. The score was 19-20 my serve and I went with no spin that was flipped aggressively–should have gone with underspin. Jan-Ove was very supportive and gracious.

Tip: Shot selection plays an important role in table tennis. Which stroke should I use and how aggressive should it be? In a split second you need to know YOUR options. Make good choices.

In 1977 our team moved into the first division at the Worlds. Then, in 1979, we were sent back to division two. Boy, that one still stings. Then, in 1981 in Novi Sad, Yugoslavia, this team won the second division again. It all came down to us versus Romania and we needed to win by 5-1, as we had lost to the Netherlands and Romania had won against them. We won 5-0, with Eric and Ricky coming through. Coach switched our regular order so I could play their #1 first. Great feeling to be back in the top division for Tokyo 1983. So important to have that to look forward to when training. L-R: Mike Bush, Scott Boggan, Me, Houshang Bozorgzadeh, Rick Seemiller, and Eric Boggan.

Tip: It's important to be a team player and be supportive no matter what your role in the team is. It's a great feeling to help a teammate out when they are down and vice versa.

Seemiller Happy To Escape North Korea

By MILTON RICHMAN
United Press International

If you have any complaint, any kick at all about this country, make sure you talk to Danny Seemiller so he can tell you about "the worst place I've ever been in my life" — North Korea.

"As soon as we left, the four other team members and I said the same thing to each other," reveals the 24-year-old U.S. table tennis national champion. "We said, 'Thank God, we're out.'"

Danny Seemiller is a bright looking youngster from Carrick who has been ranked the No. 1 table tennis player in this country for the past seven years.

Since turning professional five years ago, he has been practically everywhere in the world, including places like the Peoples' Republic of China, Japan, Russia, Yugoslavia, Czechoslovakia, Hungary, Saudi Arabia, Iran, Germany, France, Italy, Sweden and Denmark, but he says he has never been to any place like Pyongyang, North Korea, where he and the four other members of the U.S. team spent from April 22 to May 7 for the 35th World Table Tennis Championship.

"The people there don't make any secret of the way they feel about us," Seemiller says. "Right on their postage stamps, they have printed phrases like 'Down with U.S. Imperialism,' 'Yankees get out of Korea,' and 'Americans Go Home.' That's because of the American soldiers doing guard duty in the Demalitarized Zone, I suppose.

"Kim Il Sung not only is the North Koreans' governmental leader, he's their God. The people work eight hours a day, study eight hours a day, six days a week and have virtually no recreation. They live their lives for their government. That's terrible.

"We didn't come to North Korea expecting a royal welcome, but in the two weeks we were there, the people never showed us a single act of kindness," Seemmiller continued. "They shoved us and pushed us around, and anywhere we went, they always made us sit in the back. They treated us pretty much as if the war was still on and we were their enemies."

Seemiller tells this story:

"We had brought a Frisbee with us and one day we decided to play with it in the street where we were staying. I had a stereo cassette and turned it on while we were playing. That drew a crowd of

DANNY SEEMILLER
Back in the good old USA.

people who wondered what we were up to.

"The next thing you know, here comes this North Korea van with a loudspeaker playing their music very loudly over ours. This van stops right in front of us and their loudspeaker purposely drowns out the music from our stereo. One of their officials then told us we couldn't play Frisbee there. We would have to go to a specified area which they never specified."

U.S. team members and their supporters who came to North Korea with them from the states encountered obstacles everywhere they went, Seemiller said.

"There were people with us from Missouri, New Jersey and Pennsylvania, and the hotel rate for them was supposed to be $26 a day. When it came time for them to check out, though, they found they were being charged for the lamps in their room, the rugs on their floor and everything else."

The actual table tennis competition was held in one of the huge national gymnasiums in Pyongyang and on the day the North Korean team was to oppose the U.S. team, you couldn't find a seat in the place. The Americans could feel the spectators' hostility.

"There must've been 20,000 North Koreans in that building and from the way they carried on, you'd have thought it was a war instead of a table tennis match," Seemiller says.

"I never heard so much screaming in my life. It seemed like the rafters were going to come down. They beat us 5-0. The officiating was unsportsmanlike to say the least. I lost both my matches on questionable calls."

Seemiller, whose younger brother, Randy, is the third ranked table tennis player in this country, has played approximately 5,000 matches in his career and won something like 4,800 of them. He looks like Jimmy Connors and also plays like him, hitting the ball left-handed and relying heavily on aggressive, powerful strokes.

You might see him in the World Invitational Racquets championship on CBS-TV today between 2:30 and 4 p.m. But you'll never see him going to North Korea again.

"We kept counting the days until we got out," he says. "The trip changed my values about the United States. I always loved my country. Now I care for it so much more."

Our team spent 15 days in North Korea in 1979. It was uncomfortable the whole time. We had a guard 24 hours a day that was with us for security. I did not see any joy or happiness among the people. No one ever smiled or even laughed. Very memorable trip in many ways.

1985 World Team in Goteborg, Sweden. Many good memories in the first division that year. We beat Italy 5-4 to remain in the top category. I believe this photo was right after that match. The smiles are too real. This was Rick's last worlds as he retired soon after. Eric also sat out a couple of years and did not play again until 1989.

L-R: Sean O'Neill, me, Houshang Bozorgzadeh, Brian Masters, Rick Seemiller, and Eric Boggan.

Tip: Hard work is always rewarded. Practice like you play.

ダニー・シミラー 卓球講習会 防府会場

日　時　昭和54年2月19日(月)15時50分
場　所　協和醗酵工業㈱防府工場体育館
主　催　防府市体育協会.防府市教育委員会
後　援　防府市.山口県卓球協会.山口県教育委員会
主　管　防府市体育協会

ダニー・シーミラー
DANNY SEEMILLER

1976 - 77年　男子シングルス全米チャンピオン
1976 - 78年　男子ダブルス全米チャンピオン
1976 - 78年　混合ダブルス全米チャンピオン
1973 - 78年　カナダ・オープン・男子シングルス6連勝
現在全米ランキングNO.1

長谷川信彦選手

昭和022年3月5日、愛知県の瀬戸市で生まれる。

昭和44年に愛知工業大学を卒業し、その年、（株）タマスに入社。卓球レポート編集部所属、現在31才。

昭和40年の大学1年生のとき、18才の史上最年少の全日本チャンピオンになって以来、前人未踏の全日本シングルス6回優勝の史上最多優勝記録、10年連続ベスト4と決勝進出8回の新記録を樹立。また、ダブルス1回、混合複3回優勝し、優勝獲得数、計10回の史上最多優勝記録を樹立。

アジア選手権大会では、昭和42年に初出場して、団体シングルスに優勝して以来、団体戦4回、シングルス4回、ダブルス3回、混合複2回の、金メダル数、計13個を獲得。

世界選手権大会では、4回出場し、'67年ストックホルム大会で団体、シングルス、混合複の3種目に優勝。'69年ミュンヘン大会で団体、混合複の2種目に優勝。

My favorite place to train and compete was in Japan. For training, I would be at the Tokyo Butterfly Dohjo for morning and afternoon sessions. Then at night I would take the train to Meiji University and play matches there. Meiji was one of the top teams and only a 10-minute ride on the subway. Table tennis in Japan is quite popular and nearly all the schools have their own team.

Tip: For a solid shot the center of the racket is the goal. See above.

Teaching table tennis in a camp setting is one of my favorite parts of being a coach. Here's a class with so many friendly students it was memorable. My assistant, Mark Nordby on the right in the black shirt, was once a PGA golf teaching pro and an excellent TT coach. Dan Jr. is in the back with glasses.

Tip: When competing the key is to "be prepared to perform." Good warm up, stretching, and any knowledge of the opponent that may be helpful. Don't worry about winning/losing. It's important to have a strategy, then try to make it happen.

Local winners at the U.S. Open table tennis tournament included 13-year-old Dan Seemiller Jr., 11-year-old A.J. Brewer and his 7-year-old brother, C.J.

After a long playing career, coaching young players can be just as satisfying. Here are three winners from South Bend Table Tennis. A.J. and C.J. had talent for TT but were pulled away by success in baseball. A.J. reached a 2300 rating at age 12. My son, Dan Jr., is the head coach of the El Paso Table Tennis club in Texas.

Tip: Nothing can be more important than good fundamentals. How can you tell if yours are solid? Pure topspin and underspin on your counters and pushes. No sidespin on any of them. Sidespin is used by choice and should not creep into your basic strokes.

Copyright 1983 by Robert Compton

Danny Seemiller, 1982 U.S. Men's Singles Champion

My most improbable comeback, the 1982 U.S. Men's Final versus Eric Boggan. He is the favorite as he is having a great season internationally. Eric easily wins the first, 21-10, and is 20-14 up in the second. I score eight in a row to get back in the match. Now 2-2 in games and Eric leads 19-16 and serving. I win all five on his serve to win 21-19, 3 games to 2. That's how you hang in there and steal a match by never giving up.

Tip: Momentum swings in TT are huge. Keeping one's focus and staying in the present are keys to success.

Doubles play in table tennis is very challenging. Movement, shot selection, and teamwork all play a role. Lefty/Righty combination makes moving much easier. Here Rick and I are in the 1980 U.S. Open final versus Zoran Kosanovic and Ray Guillen, also a left/right pairing.

The thrill of victory. Rick hits in the winning shot in the final of the doubles at the 1980 U.S. Open in Ft. Worth. Our opponents were Zoran Kosanovic and Ray Guillen, and you can see by the final score there was some excellent drama for ESPN. Final score was 25-23 in game five, 3 games to 2.

Scott Butler (left) and Houshang Bozorgzadeh engage in an Exhibition before 15,000 mesmerized onlookers during halftime at a recent College basketball game between Iowa and Michigan. Houshang noted afterward that everyone except the concession stand owners appreciated the display. They were apparently miffed because few spectators were leaving their seats from the Exhibition, unlike during most halftimes.

Table Tennis exhibitions are exciting. A bit nerve wracking as one hopes to put on a good show. Here's our U.S. Team coach, Houshang, and Scott Butler, U.S. Pan Am team member, having some fun and promoting the sport at a sold-out basketball game between Michigan and Iowa. One of my most memorable ones was a three-day exhibition at a new mall in Phoenix. Up on the billboard was the challenge: $1,000 to anyone who can win against me in a game to 21. By Sunday, the line waiting to try was 25 players long.

Across the street from the Butterfly office building in Tokyo. The training hall is behind the office. The apartment for my use was a two-minute walk. There were always excellent partners to train with available at the Dohjo each day. Japanese players train very hard, so I had to be on my toes to keep up. One of the main difficulties is the language barrier. Without an interpreter it can get difficult at times.

U.S. Team Trials **At Caesars Palace**

U. S. MEN'S TEAM: (INSERT) HOUSHANG BOZORGZADEH, CAPTAIN, (LEFT... TO RIGHT) DANNY SEEMILLER, RICKY SEEMILLER, TEAM MANAGER JOHN READ, RAY GUILLEN, VICE PRESIDENT OF CAESARS PALACE NEIL... SMYTH, DEAN GALARDI, PAUL RAPHEL, AND ALTERNATE MIKE BUSH.

U. S. WOMEN'S TEAM: (LEFT TO RIGHT) IN-SOOK BHUSHAN, ALICE GREEN, MANAGER JOHN READ, JUDY BOCHENSKI, TEAM TRAINER PAT CROWLEY, ANGIE ROSAL, VICE PRESIDENT OF CAESARS PALACE NEIL SMYTH, ALTERNATE OLGA SOLTESZ, AND CAPTAIN HEATHER ANGELINETTA.

Many memories from Caesar's Palace 1976-1980. Neil Smyth of Caesar's made us feel like top-class athletes. Joe Louis gave out the awards! What could be better than heading to Caesar's in Las Vegas for our National TT Championships?

Tip: "Spin to Win" is a saying but it is so very true in TT. High levels of spin control the ball's flight and gives one a greater ability to vary the spin.

ACTION AT THE BENSON AND HEDGES "LOVE BIRD" TOURNAMENT IN KINGSTON, JAMAICA: IN SOOK NA BHUSHAN OF THE U.S. ON HER WAY TO BEATING JILL HAMMERSLEY, ENGLAND NO. 1.

Of all the places I've played, the crowd in Jamaica was one of the most appreciative. They really root hard, loud, and fully support the players. One of my memories from this tournament is playing Desmond Douglas in the final. Local hero. Sold-out arena. Super loud and fun.
Des had beaten me before but not that night.

Tip: If you have won 3-4 points in a row, don't be satisfied. Keep the streak going. Your opponent is likely frustrated by now so here's a chance to take it to seven, even eight straight and close out the game.

U.S. TEAM TO CALCUTTA WORLD'S: (front row, left to right) DAL-JOON LEE, LIM MING CHUI, DANNY SEEMILLER, PAUL RAPHEL; (standing, left to right): ANGELITA ROSAL, TIM BOGGAN (NPC), JUDY BOCHENSKI, OLGA SOLTESZ, PATTY MARTINEZ, AND PETER PRADIT.

On to my second World Championships. They were held every two years back then. Calcutta, India was the host. Wow, was it crowded there! Our Men's Team made it to the final of the second division, and just like '73, we lost. This time to Poland, 5-4. A heartbreaking loss. Now we have to wait until 1977 for another chance. Check out those denim outfits and flyaway collars.

Tip: One has to learn how to handle losing before they can figure out how to win.

Copyright 1981 @ Neal Fox

THAT'S OUR DANNY, OF COURSE, IN THE BUTTERFLY POSTER IN THE WINDOW OF THIS NOVI SAD SPORTING GOODS STORE. AND WELL THIS WOMAN SHOULD BE LOOKING AT HIM, FOR HE WAS AGAIN THE DRIVING FORCE BEHIND OUR SUCCESS IN TEAM PLAY. TWICE NOW HE'S LED THE U . S. MEN'S TEAM OUT OF THE SECOND DIVISION INTO THE FIRST. THIS YEAR HIS TEAM RECORD WAS 19-0—WHICH MEANS THAT IN SECOND DIVISION PLAY FROM 1975 ON, HIS RECORD IS AN AMAZING 66-1.

Playing at the worlds for the U.S. Team was my #1 goal in table tennis. My dream was to represent USA against China. Dream big and you might just get there.

Photos by George Perrett

GUESS WHO WON

Errol Caetano was the #1 Canadian in the 70s and he and I had some epic close matches. Errol was smooth and a great shot-maker.

Photo by Don Weems

DANNY SEEMILLER, MIDDLESEX OPEN WINNER.

Photo by Stewart Ansteth

MIKE VEILLETTE, '75 MICHIGAN MEN'S CHAMPION.

In 1976 brother Rick, Mike Veillette and I went on a three-week tour of Europe. First stop was the Yugoslav Open, then the Scandinavian Open in Sweden, then on to England for the Middlesex Open. A busy three weeks. The trip finished on a high note, with my win in England. On the last day of the Yugoslav Open the three of us went hiking up into the nearby mountains. We approached an area that had no trespassing allowed. Mike had a camera and they arrested us and took us to jail and placed each of us in separate cells. They accused us of taking photos of a secured facility. They took Mike's camera, checked the film, and 14 hours later they let us go. An adventure it was. Pretty damn scary too.

Tip: Ready position–mostly neutral, slightly favoring the forehand. Weight forward, on toes and focused. Excellent photo of Mike preparing to return serve.

JUNE 18-24 2018 • LAS VEGAS, NV

Table Tennis is popular worldwide. In 2018, USA Table Tennis held the World Veterans Tourney in Las Vegas. 4,000 players entered and stayed the week. Players from 97 countries were represented. There were 250 tables, all in one huge hall. The 60-64 Men's age group was the largest at almost 700 entrants.

Tip: Don't let age hold you back. Anyone can improve if they are determined to do so.

MT. OLIVER INDIANS FOOTBALL TEAM . . . will close its season on Thanksgiving Day by playing in the Allegheny County Workhouse Annual Turkey Bowl Game to be held beginning at 1 p.m. at the Workhouse. Mt. Oliver will play the Conference Champs, Mon-Yough. The Mt. Oliver Indians Football Team (pictured above) includes; Manager Pat Egan in front row holding the ball; first row l to r) Dave Hennon, Bruce Haney, Tom Herron, Rich Piels, Walt Matuszak, Dave Nath, Dave Egan, Dan Seemiller, Chris Costa, Ray Bobak, Tom Zulka; (second row l to r) John Mulvaney, Jim Kelly, Dave Pleitz, John Pope, Joe Friel, Kevin Garrett, Bill Egan, Gary Milkovich, Jim Fink, Gary Pawloski, Joe Nichy; (third row l to r) John Thompson, Bill Francis, Matt Aloisio, Don Macurak, Ron Rahenkamp, Ron Bertha, Jim Mutschler, Jerry Breisinger, Paul Thompson, and Keith Morrell.

Participating in team sports teaches one all types of important lessons. I loved playing football and baseball and all the friendships we had competing together. Photo is of the "Mt. Oliver Indians," I'm #17, front row. I was the QB and right linebacker. Many of these players in the photo went on to win the City High School Championship at Carrick High. I didn't play in high school. Coach thought I was too small and didn't give me a chance. This was one of the main reasons I started to play TT seriously.

Trip around the World. In 1979 our U.S. Team was invited to participate in the Hong Kong Invitational. We went from there to Iran. Houshang, our coach, who's from Iran, set up a one-week tour of his home country where we played matches against their National Team members. Then it was back to Dallas, Texas. for another important U.S. tourney. Photo from the Hong Kong Daily Newspaper.

USA Team marching in the Opening Ceremony at the 1981 World Championships in Novi Sad, Yugoslavia. In those days, the tournament was two weeks long. During the first week we play the teams and the second the singles and doubles events.

Tip: One of the best techniques in the sport is to play your opponent wide to the forehand and then deep and wide to the backhand.

AP Photo/CHITOSE SUZUKI

Eye on the ball

Petra Cada of Canada serves during her first-round game in table tennis women's singles against Olfa Guenni of Tunisia at the Olympic Games in Athens, Saturday.

Tip: Photo says it all. Keep your eyes on the ball and focus.

In voller Aktion. Jülichs Tischtennis-Star Danny Seemiller. Beim Training hinterließ er einen ausgezeichneten Eindruck. Heute abend hat er Premiere. (Foto: Günter Petersen)

Jülich: „Mit Danny werden wir diesmal deutscher Meister"

Tischtennis-Euphorie bei Simex – Heute gegen Altena

Playing for a team in the German Bundesliga (Julich) was one of the highlights of my career. This was the top professional league in Europe. There were six players on our team, and we had a trainer. Playing so many competitive matches and having a team to support you was invaluable. The hard part was being away from home, it can get lonely, but I knew that to keep improving, this was the next step for me.

111

South Bend's own Mark Hazinski started at the SBTTC at age 9. He made the U.S. Olympic Team in 2004 and the Pan Am Teams in 2003 and 2007. Mark also won his hometown St. Joe Valley tournament an astounding nine times. In 2009 Mark and I won the U.S. Men's Doubles title in Las Vegas. In that doubles final, against Adam Hugh and Fan Yiyong, we were up 2-1 and 4-2 when they called time. During the break I started to think about my father who passed away just a month before and started to get emotional. After the timeout we scored six in a row to pull away. What was it that made Mark special? His power could overwhelm opponents.

1982 U.S. Women's Champion In-sook Bhushan

CBS started a new sports show. It was called "Challenge of the Sexes." I was chosen to play Insook Bhushan. She was the U.S. Women's Champion. The handicap would be that she served all the time and I had to end the rally by the sixth stroke. Insook was a defensive player so it made for exciting countdowns each point as I would push two or three and then attack. The local school brought in a few hundred students to cheer us on. It was pretty loud in the gym as the girls cheered loudly for her and the boys for me. I won 2-0 and $2,500, Insook $1,250. Just after the table tennis, Jerry West, NBA Laker, played a game of horse versus a high school girl basketball player. She won.

Desmond Douglas shows the correct technique over the table. To attack the short balls one must extend the arm and step in under the table, then flip the racket forward. Don't start the stroke until you get close to the ball. Desmond was England's top player for several years and had one of the best short games (play close to the net) in the world. He also took every ball as early as possible, putting time pressure on his opponents.

Tip: What do we mean by short game? This is your ability to serve short, drop the ball short, and attack these short balls with a flip. Short would mean the first 1/3 of the table next to the net. If one is skillful in this technique, you will often get that critical first attack.

Really like this photo from the Tees Sport magazine in the 70's. In those days, the top Europeans were equal or better than the Chinese. Now China is a powerhouse that has proven difficult to break.

Attending the national sporting goods show was a staple every year, representing Butterfly. There are hundreds of booths vying for attention and our TT show always drew a crowd. Todd Sweeris, 2000 Olympian, was my partner. Each year I would go and challenge the world's best free throw shooter at his booth. This year I hit all 10 and he missed one. Free T-shirt.

Tip: It's important when teaching young players to be serious but it must be fun too. After training, play games like dodgeball, shooting baskets, relays, skill contests, doubles, and anything else.

116

Merry Christmas to all. My parents Ray and Dorothy loved sharing this special day. In 1966 my parents bought us a ping-pong table upon my request.

24 years ago I moved my family to South Bend, Indiana to become the junior program coach.
Top: These are four of the parents who had children in the program:
- Jim Lynch: Jordan and Jared
- Brad Balmer: Nicole
- Matt Hazinski: Katy, Janelle, and Mark
- Tom Clemmons: Joe

Bottom: One of our junior teams at the Detroit National Teams: Gordon Cochran, John Leach, Eli Khan, and Joey Cochran.

In 1972, after graduating high school, I moved to Grand Rapids, MI, to live and train with Dell Sweeris. After 11 months, in May, 1973, their son Todd was born, and I moved to an apartment. His room was the one I was staying in. Twenty-seven years later, in Sydney, I am coaching him in the 2000 Olympic games. Photo of David Zhuang and Todd after a big win and a photo of Khoa Nguyen and Cheng Yinghua in between games. Third photo is of the water taxi from the Olympic village to downtown Sydney. The ride into town took 15 minutes. A refreshing, visual ride on the water. I also had the chance to sit and watch a match with Bill Gates and explain to him some of the techniques being used. He likes watching table tennis but does not donate to sports or their organizations.

Having a couple of brothers to practice with and share wins and losses with made the training much easier and enjoyable. I was always an emotional player and I figure after all that hard work, when you win you might as well enjoy it for a moment or two. Sometimes when the result was clear I would try to be cool, but once I saw my brothers and friends it would just burst out.

1st photo: Randy is facing me with Rick just behind.
2nd photo: Moments after my fifth singles win.
Photos by Robert Compton.

Tip: Hard work is always rewarded and dream big. The next champion could be you.

120

	A	B	C	D	E	F	G	H	I	J	K	L		
A BOGGAN, E.	X	W 19,-16,18 Carry Ovr	W 18,11 Carry Ovr	L -17,-21	W 10,14	W 6,15	W -19,13,17	W 18,6	W 16,8	W 11,14	W 18,-19,17	W 9,5	10/1	2
B SCHWARTZBERG	L 1-2 Carry Ovr	X	W -7,12,18 Carry Ovr	L 0-2	L 0-2	W 18,17	L -7,16,16	L 1-2	W 15,-15,18	L 1-2	W 16,19	W -12,22,10	6/5	6
C BUI, Q.	L 0-2 Carry Ovr	L 1-2 7,-12,18	X	L 1-2	L 1-2	W 17,17	L 0-2	W 19,9	W 13,18	L 0-2	W 21,15	W -16,18,19	5/6	8
D SEEMILLER, D.	W 17,21	W 9,14	W -21,14,16	X	W 17,10 Carry Ovr	W -19,19,13 Carry Ovr	W 17,7	W 17,8	W 12,9	W 9,19	W 14,14	W 16,14	11/0	1
E MALEK, A.	L 0-2	W 16,14	W -19,10,16	L 0-2 Carry Ovr	X	W 11,15 Carry Ovr	L 0-2	L 0-2	W -18,11,15	L 1-2	L 0-2	W 13,15	5/6	7
F LANE, J.	L 0-2	L 0-2	L 0-2	L 1-2 Carry Ovr	L 0-2 Carry Ovr	X	L 0-2	L 0-2	L 1-2	W -18,9,15	W 15,13	L 1-2	2/9	11
G BOGGAN, S.	L 1-2	L 1-2	W 18,18	L 0-2	W 12,18	W 9,12	X	W -19,17,16 Carry Ovr	W 18,11 Carry Ovr	L 1-2	W 9,16	W 17,14	7/4	4
H MASTERS, B.	L 0-2	W -15,16,19	L 0-2	L 0-2	W 9,12	W 21,22	W -19,-17,16 Carry Ovr	X	W 21,16 Carry Ovr	L 0-2	W 14,-17,16	W 9,7	6/5	5
I NGUYEN, K.	L 0-2	L 1-2	L 0-2	L 0-2	L 1-2	W -16,20,20	L 0-2 Carry Ovr	L 0-2 Carry Ovr	X	L 0-2	W 18,18	L 1-2	2/9	10
J SEEMILLER, R.	L 0-2	W -13,17,17	W 20,8	L 0-2	W 16,-15,22	L 1-2	W 17,-19,14	W 21,8	W 7,12	X	W 12,14 Carry Ovr	W 12,21 Carry Ovr	8/3	3
K OLSON, B.	L 1-2	L 0-2	L 0-2	L 0-2	W 11,18	L 0-2	L 0-2	L 1-2	L 0-2 Carry Ovr	L 0-2 Carry Ovr	X	W 13,17 Carry Ovr	2/9	12
L GUILLEN, R.	L 0-2	L 1-2	L 1-2	L 0-2	L 0-2	W 16,-13,17	L 0-2	L 0-2	W 16,-18,16	L 0-2 Carry Ovr	L 0-2 Carry Ovr	X	2/9	9

Men's Round Robin Results

The final 12 Round Robin at the 1983 Nationals at the Tropicana Hotel in Las Vegas.

Tropicana Hotel Las Vegas, 1982 Men's final versus Eric Boggan. Where's Eric? He has kicked down the barriers and is in the deep right corner somewhere. I win a close one. Where is the ball? Can you see it? It's just above the C in the Tropicana barrier in the corner and rising. You can see the ball against the man's black pants- a white blur.
Photo by Robert Compton.

Tip: When serving, anticipation should be at a high level and being aggressive. When receiving, a more neutral stance is needed. Stay neutral, be decisive, know your options.

My annual trip to Japan took place every February and lasted about three weeks on average. In this photo I am playing an exhibition with Shigeo Itoh. Shigeo is one of the greatest players of all time. Incredible power and determination. He won the 1969 world singles and in 1971 made it to the final in his homeland Japan, losing the final to Stellan Bengtsson of Sweden. How amazing is that? I think he gets overlooked when the talk of all-time greats comes up. I watched Shigeo's match with chopper Eberhard Schöler, the world men's singles final, on ABC Wide World of Sports that Saturday in 1969, and it was thrilling. Down 0-2 in games and losing the third, he came back to win 3-2. What changed, I asked him? He said he switched from a power looping game to a high spin control loop that Eberhard had trouble keeping low. Shigeo cried uncontrollably when handed the singles trophy. Very moving and great TV.

Tip: Heavy spin can neutralize any opponent.

Table tennis is a lifetime sport. One can play as a child or a senior and any age in between. In 2018, The World Veterans Championships were held in Las Vegas with 4,000 competitors from 97 countries. Veteran is anyone over 40.

Tip: Always keep working to improve your technique. Don't just blindly practice and expect to improve.

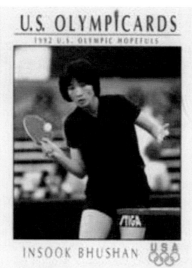

In 1988 table tennis made its Olympic debut in Seoul. I lost a close 3-2 match to Sean O'Neill as there was only one spot for America. In 1992 I won the U.S. trials but faltered in the Continental trials with Canada. Because the Olympics has too many athletes, they do not have many slots for TT to qualify, so we have to go by continent. North America has three Olympic slots so we must play a continental trial to earn the right to compete at the Olympic Games.

Good times at the U.S. Open in Milwaukee a few years back. Michael Gopin (on the right) and I had just won the 4200 doubles event. Mark Hazinski, 2004 Olympian and 4x runner-up at the U.S. Nationals, with our good friend and America's finest U.S. coach, Mark Nordby. Mark coached all three of us and taught us so much. We miss you Mark. You made us all better for knowing you. Mark passed away in 2016. Mark Nordby was a professional PGA golf teacher. This is how he was so adept at teaching and coaching. When he switched to table tennis, the concepts he learned were invaluable to all his students. Plus you knew he cared–the essential ingredient of a great coach.

Larry Hodges' book "Table Tennis Tactics for Thinkers" is the best one on the market. He has authored nine table tennis books (he says he has more coming), but this is my favorite. Larry is a member of the USATT Hall Of Fame and the 2018 USATT Lifetime Achievement Award Winner.

Many memories from South Park TTC where I grew up and learned the game. I don't remember everyone in the photo. Many of these players copied my style of play with anti-spin on one side. I will always remember Thursday night league!

1st row, 2nd from left: Jim Armocida, next to him Brian Rodgers.

2nd row: Behrooz Behnam, 4th Stan Carrington–love you Stan, Gary Egri–hardest worker ever, Bill Walk and sons Dan and Mike, Tom Pratt, Bob Doby- my man.

3rd row: Rick Claraval–the looper, Jim Neal from West Virginia, Tim Seemiller, Gary Falce, Jamie Veltri, Barry Rodgers (club president), Larry Lowry and sons Steve and Dave, not sure, me, Jeff Kearns, Perry Schwartzberg, and Marla Jonas.

Back row: Mr. Ramirez, 5th one Alex Meleshenko, 7th one Chip Coulter, and at the end Ken Milgram.

1985 Worlds in Goteborg, Sweden. Great tourney. Here I am in the 9th match versus Italy. Score is 4-4 in matches and this is the final one. I win and this keeps the U.S. in the first division. Playing for the U.S. team was always a thrill.

When a man gazes at a mountain, it has been said that there is a subconscious urge to lift it up, and so the mountain becomes a great source of strength. When Danny Seemiller first picked up a table tennis paddle, no one ever imagined that he might become the greatest athlete in the history of the game. But the domination of table tennis by athletes of other countries became a great source of strength for Danny. Now, Danny Seemiller is about to lift that mountain. When he does, it should be a tremendous source of pride for America.

This is what happens when you have an agent. I had a couple of agents during my career. This one was Baldy Regan and he was a magistrate in Pittsburgh. He knew everybody and liked to bring me along to these parties and gatherings as he was closely connected to the Steeler football team. It was a fun time. We used these promotional folders mostly for mall and school exhibitions. The chicken is in reference to the coop we renovated to train in.

130

I got a little excited after winning the fourth game, now 2-2, against world #2 in Tokyo 1983. It was always my dream to beat the Chinese at the World Championships. The reason I was extra motivated is Cai Zhenhua was very disrespectful to me early on in the match. He was always like that with other players, but no one ever took him up on it. Two times early on I popped up his serve and he loop killed, and he did a full 360. I walked right up to him and said if you ever do that again.....I'll leave it at that. I led 10-8 in game five before losing, after a 20-minute delay on a fault serve called on Cai that was eventually taken away by the referee. The Chinese always got their way. Check out Cai walking somberly in the background. When the main referee, not the umpire of the match, changed the score back from 11-8 to 10-8 I lost my focus. Cai was nervous before the break and I was nervous after.

This is one of my favorites for sure, the 1983 Nationals final versus my rival Eric Boggan. The match was a 2/3 and I was leading 1-0 and 13-5. Eric sort of gave up and whacked in two winners. Next thing I know I'm down 20-19. I realize if I lose this game my chances go down to 25% or less. I deuce it, but Eric again gets the ad, 21-20. One of my proudest moments in this sport as I play three perfect points to win. On the last one, Eric served FH and looped down the line. I was able to block it wide to his FH as Eric scrambled and threw his paddle at the ball– didn't get there in time. Second place I think was $1,250, with first $3,000. I also had a $5,000 bonus from Butterfly. Only time I ever jumped on the table, but I loved it. Eric's reaction is priceless. This was my fifth singles title. Eric had beaten my brother Rick in the semis. Photo by Robert Compton.

A dream come true. My brother Rick and I practiced for years in our backyard chicken coop–renovated–to someday beat the Chinese. In 1977, round of 16, we did it. The score was 3-0 against the #1 seed and two-time world singles champion Guo Yue Hua and his partner Liao Fu Min. The match was in Birmingham, England, and technically we haven't won until the ball hits the floor. After the match we were so thrilled we were hoping that maybe someone caught this moment on camera. This was the World Championships. Rick and I won eight U.S. doubles championships in a row, 1976-1983.

Here is a memorable photo. Probably my most satisfying win in my career. The 1982 National final against Eric Boggan. Eric was just coming off a fantastic first half of the season in the German league. In game one my defensive mix did not work. Eric had really improved his loop and offense, 21-10. In game two more of the same as Eric leads 20-14. Things are looking bleak. At 20-15 my serve I decide to forgo the defense and attack his FH relentlessly. I'm on a roll and it's 20-20. Obviously, I NEED this game. Eric serves off! Another series of loops and it's one game apiece. Whew! I use that momentum to secure the third game and lead 13-10 in game four, when Eric scores seven in a row and it is now 2-2. In game five there is no separation at all, 15-15. My serve. I play a bad series and go down 19-16. Eric at this time does a little sort of victory dance in the back court. I'm thinking this isn't over. He's too fired up and my thought was his serve will drift long and I can attack. 19-17. Now no way I can let him on the offense, and I hit three loops and it's now 19-18. Eric serves off. As I go back to pick up the ball, I have two thoughts. Thank goodness I was able to tie this up without hitting a shot at this most critical moment. Second thought, he's in serious trouble, don't need to do anything rash. Just keep it on the table. My plan was usually to go to the FH, but he knows that. This may be the right time to play one deep to his favored BH, and it works. 19-20. Eric can hardly breathe at this time–could you? He sets up in his BH corner to serve, then goes to the FH side. It's clear he has no plan. I'm definitely going to the forehand now. He misses my return and it's over. I've just scored five in a row to win. My emotions were true elation as my brothers Randy and Rick rush the court. Photo by Robert Compton.

Outside our hotel in Pyongyang, North Korea. You see that welcome sign in the background?
I don't believe that was true for our team.

LOSING EFFORT — Carrick's Danny Seemiller plays a close but losing match against Hong Chol of North Korea during the World Table Tennis Championships at Pyongyang, the North Korean capital. Chol edged Seemiller, 21-19, 20-22, 21-18. In later action, Seemiller took two of three matches from French opponents.

Associated Press

Can't read the caption? It says: Carrick's Danny Seemiller plays a close but losing match against Hong Chol of North Korea during the World Table Tennis Championships at Pyongyang, the North Korean Capital. Chol edged Seemiller, 21-19, 20-22, 21-18. In later action, Seemiller took two of three matches from French opponents.

Absolutely incredible happenings in North Korea in 1979 at the World Championships. Here I am playing a North Korean player. 22,000 people are cheering for him in this huge facility. This was more of a cultural war than a table tennis match. Score one game each and 18-18. I loop one and he blocks long–as I go to pick up the ball, I hear this huge cheer. The North Korean umpire has given my opponent the point. Whoa–blatant cheating. I refuse to play. The crowd starts to jeer me–all 22,000. There is a man in the third deck who has an American flag, and he lights it on fire to the cheering of the raucous crowd. I still refuse to play but realize the other 15 tables in the hall cannot play until this gets settled. So I play on and lose, 21-18. The whole time we were in North Korea we were treated differently than every other team. They watched our every move and had guards wherever we went. As a result, our play suffered, and we fell back to the second division. Now it will be four more years until we make it back to the first division, which we did. Later on, I and three others decided to stand up for this treatment and we paid them back. We took down a huge photo of Kim Il Sung and hid it under the stairwell. Thank goodness no security cameras in the hotel in 1979.

From the Worlds (Goteberg). Forehand serve in doubles play.

Playing Milan Orlowski, European Champion, at the 1985 World Championships.

U.S. Table Tennis Team

2007 Pan American Games
Rio de Janeiro, Brazil

One of my favorite teams to coach. Pan Am Games In Rio 2007 with Mark Hazinski, Han Xiao, and Eric Owens. They gave it their all in the semifinals versus Argentina. We even had two match points to advance to the gold medal match, but lost 3-2. Brazil was waiting in the final with a sell-out crowd that we would have loved to have played in front of. This was a hard defeat as coach and as a player. All three played well.

LaSalle Intermediate Academy sixth-grader A.J. Brewer, left, coaches his younger brother, Kennedy Primary Center Academy third-grader C.J. Brewer.

This is a cute photo of two of my students-brothers coaching each other at a tourney. These two were super players but they both got involved with baseball in high school and we lost them. Whenever one of my students beats me in a league or tournament match for the first time, I give them $100. AJ was 12 when he won the $100. They only receive this the first win, otherwise I'd be broke. The night AJ beat me was memorable as there were a couple kids in the school, and they were wandering around the halls, so I had to throw them out. The one boy pulled the fire alarm in retaliation. Long night. The next day I went to the school and the security cameras showed the encounter and the youngster was disciplined.

Every team wants to be in the elite division at the World Championships. There are 16 in each division. In 1973, USA lost to Romania in Division Two, and so didn't advance to Division One, and in 1975 we lost to Poland 5-4 and we did not advance. Each time it takes four years to move back up. The World Championships were every two years back then. In 1977 we are playing Italy to achieve our dream. It's not going so well. We are down 4-2 and I am down 1-0 and 5-2 to their #1, Stefano Bosi. I change my tactics and start to return the serve with an anti-roll that works, and I come back 2-1 ... 4-3 Italy. Stefano was my only loss in 1975 and it almost happened again. Ray Guillen was now up versus their #3. Ray wins the eighth with masterful play, and Rick is up in the ninth versus Italy's #2 Massimo Costantini. Rick plays perfect TT and using his serve well wins easily 5-4 for the USA. Rick had lost to their #3 and Ray had lost to their #2. Now they both win. Sports can be so brutal, and the losses are tough to take, but moments like this are what the training was for. We believed it. We achieved it. There were at least 75 Americans there cheering us on in Birmingham, England and when we won, we made a lot of noise. The next worlds would be 1979 in Pyongyang, North Korea. Yikes!

Here's the winning team versus Italy: Rick, Ray, me, this young upstart, new to the team, Eric Boggan–notice how he holds the paddle–and coach Houshang.

Butterfly found some photos of my match with world #2 Cai Zhenhua. I was 28 at the time. Toughest loss I ever had. So close.... leading 10-8 in game five and the umpire faults Cai to make it 11-8, but the Chinese complain, and after a 20-minute delay, the point was taken away, 10-8. Lost my focus.

Tip: Preparing to return serve. Stay neutral. Know your options and be decisive.

FH jump smash from the 1978 U.S. Open Men's final in Oklahoma City. My opponent is Norio Takashima from Japan, the world's best defensive player and ranked #3 in the world. My big worry was my shoulder–more specifically, my tricep muscle–it was so sore I could not sleep the night before and could not lift my arm over my head. Why? I had to play so many defensive players in the teams, double, and singles. PBS, national TV, was filming the final and I was so worried I would have to default. Takashima could embarrass me if I can't loop. I was able to play, losing a 3-1 decision. Photo by Neal Fox.

Forehand loop off heavy underspin. Start low, create racket speed, finish high, and brush the ball well.

Here is a photo from The World Racquets Championships in 1978. They held this for three years, 1978-1980, on CBS, sponsored by Bristol/Myers. Each competitor had to play the other racquet sports, just not their own. I was mostly a baseball, football, and basketball athlete growing up and didn't play any racquet sports except TT, so I was in a little trouble. But I did well in racquetball, squash, tennis, and badminton. Finished in fourth place. I think I beat out the badminton player and won $5,000. Prize money was very good. First prize was $35,000.
L-R: Bjorn Borg, Flemming Delfs, Charlie Brumfield, me, and Sharif Khan.

OFFICIAL

Rick on the left and Randy on the right. Versions of our backhand. Others who used this grip were Eric Boggan, Brian Masters, Dan Seemiller Jr., Mike Walk, Chip Coulter, Tim Seemiller, Steve Lowry, Rich Burnside, Dan Walk, Ronnie Coleman, Dion Payne-Miller, and the Canadian girl Marie-Christine Roussy.

South Park Club TT Members and fellow golfers who use the "Seemiller Grip".
L to R: Chip Coulter, Mike Walk, Randy Seemiller, and Me.

Tip: 1997 U.S. Open short no-spin serve down the line. Use your legs to help keep the bounce low.

Tip: Forehand from the Backhand corner. Using your body will help you make adjustments if you are late or in a bad position.

Not always competitors! It was a pleasure announcing table tennis and analyzing the game for the viewers. Sean O'Neill, my fellow 5x U.S. Men's Singles Champion, and I have worked together several times. We once did a 10-day stint at the ESPN studios in Bristol, Connecticut, announcing live action from the Beijing, China Worlds in 1995. This was a change in our sleep patterns as we went live on the air at 10pm and went until 9am each night and early morning.

Everyone needs a rival to reach their best. Eric did that for me, and I him. We played in five U.S. Finals. He stunned me in '78 as a 15 year old, and I got him back in '82 when I made a huge comeback to win. Eric and I always got along both on the table and off. Houshang was a fine coach. Always there and ready and informative with plenty of enthusiasm. He always worried about his height. Notice he is on his toes! Houshang is in his 80s and lives just up the street from my daughter and grandkids in Longmont, Co., near Denver.

Each year our sponsor, Butterfly, would invite Rick and I to the Western Japan Open. We would train in Japan for a month or so and travel around Japan with Nobuhiko Hasegawa and Shigeo Itoh and visit clubs and give exhibition matches. Hasegawa was the 1967 world singles champ and Itoh the 1969 champ, and we learned many things from them. Each night I would take on one of them and Rick the other, and then doubles. We would then play the local top players and after the traditional party. Here I am playing doubles with Hasegawa.

Here's our training facility for many years! It was once a chicken coop and we fixed it up and it was called the "Barn." This was located about 50 yards behind our home in Pittsburgh. No air-conditioning and smelly kerosene heat in the winter.

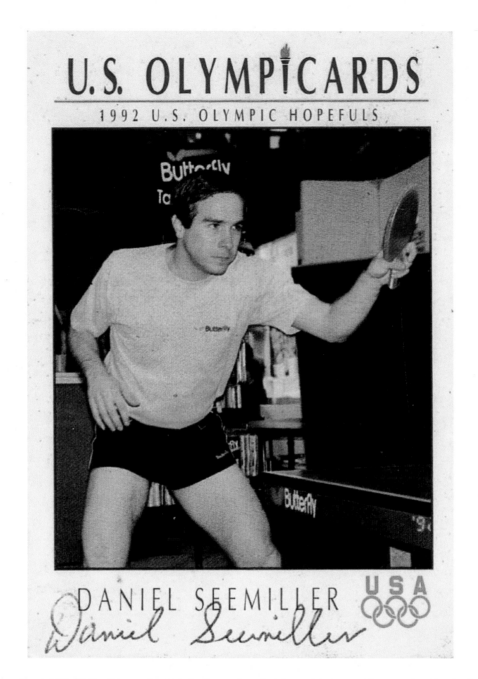

U.S. OLYMPICARDS

1992 U.S. OLYMPIC HOPEFULS

DANIEL SEEMILLER USA

By winning the 1992 U.S. Olympic Trials I received this card. Part of a set that included the Dream Team for basketball. Unfortunately, I still had to make it through the continental qualifier against the Canadians, and I didn't do well. Jim Butler won first place and by doing so the U.S. was granted the doubles team for North America. I did give Jim his only loss in the tourney. I had hopes to be Jim's selection to be his partner, but they went with Sean who had also qualified in singles. Very disappointed in that decision/choice.

Brother versus brother in the 1996 Olympic Trials in Flint, Michigan. Randy is on the far side. No fun playing one's brother anytime, but especially in the Olympic Trials. This was in a round robin so not an elimination match.

Here is one of our many after parties in Japan. Nobuhiko Hasegawa, 1967 world champion, second from left on the bottom. Just behind him to the right is Hikosuke Tamasu, the founder of Butterfly Table Tennis company. On the far right–bottom row–is Shigeo Itoh, 1969 world champion and 1971 runner-up. Pass around the Sake, rice wine.

Thanks to Butterfly TT, my sponsor for many years, my brother Rick and I used to travel to Colorado Springs, Co., and train at the Olympic Training Center. The high altitude–6,035 above sea level–made practice helpful as the thin air quickens up the game and speeds up the hands. Many of the top players have participated there. The housing, food, and coaching were provided, and the food was available all day and quite good. The playing facilities there are also excellent and being around the many different sports' athletes made one want to train. Also, having everything within five minutes walking made the training more efficient. The use of the Olympic training center has slowed because now they charge a daily fee. Above is a photo of the Resident Training Program players from Fall, 1989.

The Challenge of the Sexes ™

Trademark of Trans World International Inc.

The Challenge Of The Sexes will be televised and your entrance constitutes your consent for use of your likeness on television.

BILLIARDS
TABLE TENNIS
GYMNASTICS
BASKETBALL

6:00 p.m.
Monday, November 10, 1975
Mission Viejo High School Gym
25025 Chrisanta Drive
Mission Viejo, California

$3.75 adults
$1.50 children No refunds

N⁰   192

Here's an event from way back in 1975. The Challenge of the Sexes was held in California and telecast on CBS. My opponent was Insook Bhushan, 11-times U.S. Women's Singles Champion. In each event there was a spot. Mine was that Insook would serve all the time and I would have to win the point by my sixth shot. With Insook being a defender, the rallies often went to that sixth shot. It was great fun as I won 2-0. If I had lost maybe not so much fun.

Here's a photo from the Junior Olympics in Des Moines, Iowa in 2004. Table Tennis has many brothers that play. The key is having them get along so when they are home, they practice well there and help each other. No easy task. Over the years our South Bend Junior team has participated in several Junior Olympics in Charlotte, N.C., Baton Rouge, La. Detroit, Mi., Hampton Roads, Va., Knoxville, Tn., and Des Moines, Ia.

L-R: AJ Brewer, CJ Brewer, Spenser Lane, Shelby Lane
Back: Kevin Schulz, Gordon Cochran, Joe Cochran, Andre Khailo, Dan Seemiller Jr., and Dan Seemiller Sr.

Tip: If you don't have a big forehand topspin loop that has range it will be very hard to improve.

My first camp was a Dell Sweeris camp in Grand Rapids, Michigan. I learned many new techniques that week and it was hard work, but fun. Hosting camps in the summer kept us busy and in shape. This was in 1980.

Being on the U.S. Team means one gets invited to many countries. Here is a visit I had to the Dominican Republic with my U.S. Teammate Fuarnado Roberts. Fuarnado was a defensive player. It was a treat to watch him in action. I remember the two youngsters in the photo as very good players. We gave a clinic and trained with the best they had. Always a good sweat in the heat and humidity of the Caribbean. Hans was the sponsor for the seven-day visit.
L-R: Juan Vila, me, Hans Hieronimus, Fuarnado Roberts, and Rolando Fermin.

Here's the South Bend TTC Junior team for 2019-2020. They all have big loops and are looking forward to training and playing in the Thursday night league when we reopen. Looks more like a wrestling team!

L-R: Dan Seemiller Sr., Dominique Clark, Marty Stoner, Dion Payne-Miller, Ronnie Coleman.

 **USA Table Tennis Team
Games of the XXVIII Olympiad
Athens, Greece**

One of the great treasures of being a coach is to see your student progress and learn to be the best they can be. I started coaching Mark Hazinski when he was 11 years old. That's him at a clinic in South Bend, In., front row, fourth from the right, in blue shirt. In the top photo Mark makes the Olympic team in 2004 to Athens, Greece and I am nominated as the coach.

The 1996 Olympics were in Atlanta, and GM was one of the major sponsors. Sean O'Neill and I both tried out for the team and didn't make it. Because we were available, Sean, me, Eric Owens, and Scott Preiss were chosen for a GM tour that had us visiting a dozen or more factories and giving demonstrations across America. Sean and I went west through Michigan, Illinois, Iowa, Oklahoma, Texas, Louisiana and finally Georgia. Eric and Scott went east. At each factory there would be a huge tent set up outside the entrance in the parking lot and the employees were encouraged to visit on their break, lunchtime, or after work. Lots of free stuff, other demos, and Olympic games memorabilia for those that stopped by. Even though we didn't make the team, this was a great consolation prize. This was a two-month tour with a one-week break after the first month finished. Thank you, GM and Sean.

Top players from the early 1970's.

My backhand serve has been hard for my opponents to read over the years. It's a quick action with either side underspin or side topspin. In the photo on top I am attempting a side-under serve. Notice how flat the racket is. On the bottom is a side-topspin with the racket face more square.

Tip: Always read the spin on every approaching ball. You don't have to be perfect. Just make the read, and when you are wrong, remember what happened and learn from it.

Having a unique serve is valuable. My brothers, Rick and Randy, used the windshield wiper serve to trouble many opponents. Gripping the paddle with the thumb and forefinger and bending the knees at contact produces an unusual sidespin that is hard to read and difficult to handle. I never used this serve as it was too hard on my knees. Pressing down with the legs helps create more spin. Use the forefinger to wipe the racket head across and down on the ball. One of the keys to a great serve is getting the body involved like Rick does with his squat. Randy is playing with Mike Bush, former U.S. Team member.

My three heroes in table tennis growing up were Nobuhiko Hasegawa, 1967 world champ, Shigeo Itoh, 1969 world champ, and Stellan Bengtsson, 1971 world champ. Here I am playing Itoh in the red at one of our exhibitions and playing Hasegawa in the Western Japan final. Great experience and a childhood dream come true. Sadly, Nobuhiko was killed by a falling tree that he and his students were clearing to make a running track. RIP champ. 😟

Being honored at the County office downtown Pittsburgh with the three Commissioners. The proclamation was a "Table Tennis Day," named for the Seemiller brothers in Pittsburgh. You can see we are all excited...

L-R: Randy, Me, Rick, and Tim with my Dad Ray in the back. I also have two older brothers and three sisters. The County helped our club with a facility and a good rate on the Community College gym to host big tournaments.

Spirited Fighter Danny Seemiller
--- Seemiller Fights Hard Against Cai ---

About 5,000 spectators were glued to the No.16 table of the northwest of the arena. In the second round of the men's singles, a U.S. pro Danny Seemiller, 28, troubled a lot world No.2 player and the current Chinese national champion, Cai Zhenhua who's favored to bag the men's singles title. Playing a breath-taking match, Danny was almost to cause a major upset in the men's singles competition.

Danny is a U.S. national triple winner, but his world ranking is about fiftieth. The U.S. champion challenged Cai very aggressively by showing plenty of fight. Against Cai's varied service, Danny answered it hard to win a point with a decisive third-ball smash. Whenever he scored a point, he jumped up high and took a 'guts-showing' pose while while running about the court.

On the other hand, overwhelmed by Danny's fight and intensity, Cai lost the second and the fourth games and was very tense. In the final game, Danny was leading him 10-8. When we began to expect a major upset, an "accident" happened. Their umpire warned Cai that making so much noise by stamping the floor was in violation of the rule. The Chinese team protested against this and the game was interrupted for about five minutes. Due to this interruption, the stream of the contest changed favorably for Cai. After resuming the game, Cai successfully regained calmness, thus leading his opponent to easy mistakes in order to defeat him in the end.

"Thinking too much during the intermission, I have got nervous. I had protested against Cai's stamping of the floor beforehand. It's funny for the umpire to take it up at such a time," said Danny who missed a real great chance.

Danny was no doubt the very leading player of that day. Since he has had a hard time against Japanese top players, people here were surprised at his good performance against the Chinese. Danny's spirited fight and audience-attracting play made us feel something strong about him that Japanese players do not have.

**photos and article from the Asahi dated May 8,1983.(The Asahi has the largest circulation among the Japanese newspaper.)

My coach from Butterfly sent me this article.

173

After a long playing career–25 years–I became the U.S. National Men's Team coach in 1999 and continued for 10 years until 2009. Coaching at the World Championships and the Olympic games was a thrilling experience and traveling worldwide with the team was an honor. One of my best memories was coaching at the Sydney Olympics in 2000. A lasting memory will always be marching in with the team at the Opening Ceremonies in front of 110,000 spectators. The Australian team came in right behind us and you can just imagine the excitement from the crowd. The roar brought tears to my eyes. When I wanted to go to downtown Sydney from the Olympic Village, there was a water taxi or a bus. The water taxi was my choice and what a beautiful ride down the waterways into the city it was.

Top photo, front row: Alice Green and Connie Sweeris; **back**: Dell Sweeris, me, and George Braithwaite.
2nd photo: Coaching AJ Brewer, with CJ watching.

Tip: It is an important step in one's development to have a coach to interact with and learn. Bad habits are hard to break. It is especially helpful if the coach also plays. Table tennis is a highly complex sport. Good fundamentals will build a strong foundation. Dell Sweeris was my coach for several years. Connie, Alice, and George were all on the U.S. Team that first went to China in 1971.

Having a unique serve can be a valuable weapon. Here we see two special ones. Lu Yuan Sheng preparing for the windshield wiper serve. Using one's body will help control and add energy to a quality serve.

In the second photo, Isao Nakandakare performs the tomahawk serve.

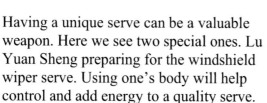

In 1975 I traveled by myself to Sweden for the SOC Open. I had a 9 am match versus a Japanese team member. I couldn't sleep and looking out my window at 5:30am, I saw a figure exercising in the parking lot. It was my Japanese opponent, Nakandakare.

L-R: Don Hayden, Phil Schmucker, me, Paul George. When I moved to South Bend, Indiana, these three men were very helpful in my table tennis endeavors.

Dragutin Surbek, European Champion and 3x world semi-finalist, shows the shakehand grip. This grip is used by 90% of players.

Photos 2&3: Li Zhenshi,2x world doubles champion and U.S. team coach 1990-95, demonstrates the athleticism needed to attack with the forehand from the backhand corner. Li is using the penhold grip.

The North American Championships held at Notre Dame University. U.S.A. versus Canada.
Poster by Paul George

37th ST JOSEPH VALLEY OPEN

at University of Notre Dame

May 26th & 27th, 2001

South Bend, IN

#	EVENT	FEE	TIME			1st	2nd	3rd - 4th	5th - 8th	9th - 16th
01	**Open**	$ 30	SAT	11:00	AM	**$5000**	**$2500**	**$1000**	**$500**	**$ 200**
02	Open Doubles	15 ea	SAT	4:30	PM	500	300	150	--	
03	Women	20	SAT	10:30	AM	200	100	50	--	
04	Hardbat - Open	15	SUN	10:30	AM	200	100	50	--	
05	Hardbat - U - 2000	15	SAT	6:00	PM	100	50	25	--	
06	Over - 40	15	SAT	2:30	PM	125	100	50	--	
07	Over - 50	15	SUN	1:30	PM	100	50	25	--	
08	U - 2550 RR	15	SUN	11:30	AM	200	100	50		
09	U - 2400 RR	15	SAT	9:00	AM	200	100	50		
10	U - 2300 RR	15	SAT	3:00	PM	150	100	50		
11	U - 2200 RR	15	SUN	9:00	AM	150	100	50		
12	U - 2100 RR	15	SAT	12:00	PM	150	100	50		
13	U - 2000 RR	15	SUN	11:30	AM	100	75	40		
14	U - 1900 RR	15	SAT	9:00	AM	100	75	40		
15	U - 1800 RR	15	SAT	3:00	PM	100	75	40		
16	U - 1675 RR	12	SUN	9:00	AM	T	T	T		
17	U - 1550 RR	12	SUN	11:30	AM	T	T	T		
18	U - 1400 RR	12	SUN	1:30	PM	T	T	T		
19	U - 1200 RR	12	SAT	9:00	AM	T	T	T		
20	U - 1000 RR	12	SAT	12:00	PM	T	T	T		
21	U - 800 RR	12	SUN	9:00	AM	T	T	T		
22	U - 12 Boys	8	SAT	10:30	AM	T	T	T		
23	U - 12 Girls	8	SAT	10:30	AM	T	T	T		
24	U - 15 Boys	8	SUN	10:30	AM	75	50	T		
25	U - 15 Girls	8	SUN	10:30	AM	T	T	T		
26	U - 18 Boys	8	SAT	2:30	PM	100	50	25		
27	U - 18 Girls	8	SAT	2:30	PM	T	T	T		
28	U - 4000 Dbls	10 ea	SAT	6:30	PM	120	80	--		
29	U - 3400 Dbls	10 ea	SAT	6:30	PM	100	60	--		

ENTER EARLY enter early ENTER EARLY enter early ENTER EARLY enter early
LIMITATIONS WILL BE PLACED BY EVENT & IN TOTAL PARTICIPANTS
DEADLINE for ENTRY is MAY 15th (but I wouldn't wait to the last minute!!)
Play on 50 PROFESSIONAL TABLES with ONE of MANY UNCOUNTED BALLS!!
Sponsored by the South Bend Parks & Recreation Department Table Tennis Club

TOURNAMENT INFORMATION

PLAYING SITE
University of Notre Dame
Joyce Athletic Center
South Bend, IN.
Players using this entry blank will be sent directions & map
with tournament & motel locations.

TOURNAMENT DIRECTOR	**Dan Seemiller**
TOURNAMENT REFEREE	**Chris Williams**

TOURNAMENT COMMITTEE

Brad Balmer	Jason Denman	Phil Schmucker

ELIGIBILITY

St. Joe Valley is open to USATT members or those who join.
All age event cutoffs will be 05/26/01.
Events #4 & #5 - A legal "hardbat" for the purposes of Event #4 must comply with
the Laws of Table Tennis Rule 2.4.3.1. The red / black Laws of Table Tennis
Rule 2.4.6 shall not apply. This event does not count for rating points.

NOTES:
1) Tournament management may modify, combine, or cancel events, limit
   entries & assign temporary rating for unrated players.
2) Draws WITHIN a round robin may be modified to avoid state / club duplication,
   but no modifications will be made BETWEEN round robin events.
3) All USATT rules will be enforced.
4) Events starting after 4 PM on Saturday MAY carryover final rounds to Sunday.
5) Entry Limitations - PLEASE DO NOT:
   enter 2 rated events with same starting time OR more than 6 total events.
6) Unrated players may enter any event (except rated doubles).
   HOWEVER , they will not advance from their Round Robin!!
7) Ratings will be from the most current listing provided by the USATT.
8) Any questions regarding the tournament, eligibility, or entry should be directed
   to Dan Seemiller at (219) 654-7476 between 6:00 PM and 9:30 PM EST.

Motel 6	Econo Lodge
52624 US 31 (Use exit 77 off of Indiana Toll Road) South Bend, IN	3233 Lincolnway West South Bend, IN
(219) 272-7072 $49.95 / Single or Double	**(219) 232-9019 or (800) 424-4777** $45.00 / Single or Double

Tell them rooms are for the Table Tennis Tournament!!

* These hotels have agreed to set aside rooms until 04/25/01 for the St. Joseph Valley Open. The rooms will be released after that date so please take advantage of their support and reserve your room AS SOON AS POSSIBLE!! *

37th ANNUAL ST. JOSEPH VALLEY OPEN ENTRY BLANK

Mail entry to:	Circle events entered:

Dan Seemiller
P.O. Box 608
New Carlisle, IN 46552

Circle events entered:
1 2 3 4 5 6 7 8 9 10 11 12 13 14
15 16 17 18 19 20 21 22 23 24 25 26 27 28 29

Name _____
Street _____
City _____ State _____ ZIP _____ Phone ( )
Birthdate _____ USATT exp. date _____ Rating _____
Doubles Partner: Open/D _____
                 U - 4000/D _____
                 U - 3400/D _____
Your club's name _____

Event fees	$	
Registration fee		3.00
Rating fee		3.00
USATT membership fee		
(Player pass $6 / Adult - 1 year $25 / Junior - 1 year $15)		
T-Shirts $12.00 (circle size) S M L XL		
Juniors Team Donation		
	TOTAL ENCLOSED $	

Checks payable to:
South Bend TTC

DO NOT MARK

Ck #		Spent		Ready to
Deposited		Verified		File

*Please enter me in the circled events. I agree to comply with all USATT regulations. I accept full
responsibility for my participation and relieve the sponsors & the USATT of any liability resulting
from injury to myself or damage to my property.*

Signature _____
(Parents sign for minors)

DEADLINE:
TUESDAY, MAY 15, 2001

Sponsored by Newmar RV company, the 2001 St. Joe Valley drew 286 participants who competed for $20,000 in prize money.

Every year for the past 22 our friends from Michigan and Pennsylvania get together for a weekend of golf. We play Ryder Cup like matches and the competition is friendly and so much fun. Our outing is called 2MuchFun, and we usually incorporate a night of table tennis on Saturday evening. Photo by Mike Veillette.

1983 Butterfly Calendar

My visit to Japan each year was in February. It was quite an honor to be on the Butterfly worldwide calendar.

My mixed doubles partner and friend Hall of Famer Patty Martinez-Wasserman.

In 2019 CBS News came to the U.S. Open in Ft. Worth, Texas to do a story on my attempt to make the U.S Olympic Team in 2020 Tokyo. Here I am playing CBS correspondent Omar Villafranca. To see the special just Google: "CBS Morning News Dan Seemiller." The segment is 4:35 in length. This was on the morning national news.

Actor/Comedian Judah Friedlander is an avid TT player who wears hats with different sayings on them. In this episode of 30 Rock he wears this hat during the show.

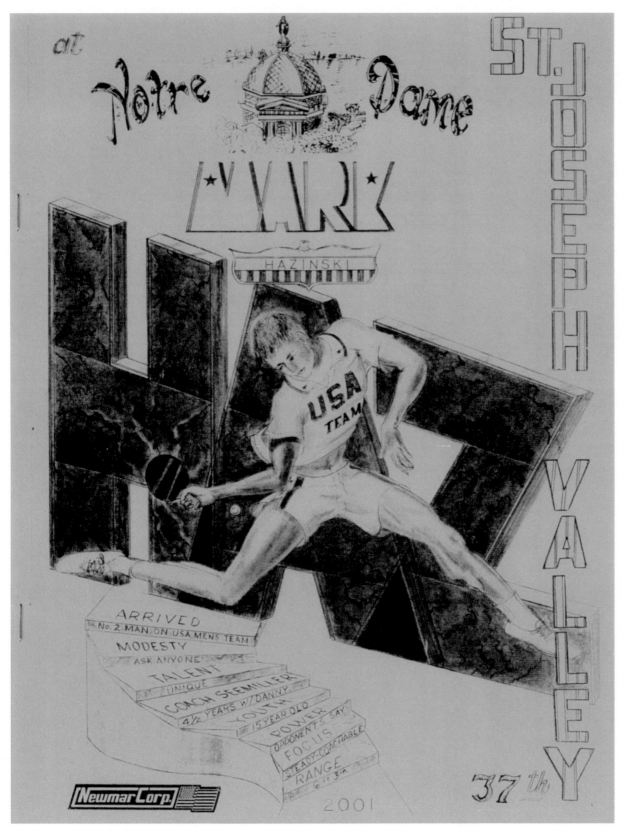

Paul George made posters for all the participants in our big annual tournament at Notre Dame. This one was of Mark Hazinski, who at the age of 15 made the U.S. Team.

Doubles champions of the Phoenix Open. Dan Seemiller Jr., coach at El Paso table tennis and Michael Gopin owner and big supporter of the sport.

The El Paso Table Tennis Club was the home of my friend
and fellow coach Mark Nordby. Mark passed away in 2016.

Continuing the Seemiller family tradition……. Dan Jr. is a full-time player and coach at the El Paso TTC.

Doubles play with my brother Rick at Las Vegas Nationals on ESPN.
Photo by Robert Compton.

Tip: For doubles, one player should play a set-up role and the other the power shots. Be alert, move well, communicate, and trust your partner.

Visiting my grandchildren, Ronan and Oona, in Colorado.

Table Tennis Team
2003 Pan American Games
Santo Domingo, Dominican Republic

The Pan Am Games was always a first-rate event. We all had a great time in the excellent weather and the friendly people of the Dominican Republic.
Front, L-R: Bob Fox (manager), Jasna Reed, Gao Jun, Lily Yip, Tawny Banh.
Back, L-R: Doru Gheorghe (women's coach), David Zhuang, Mark Hazinski, Eric Owens, Dan Seemiller (men's coach)

It was a great honor to accept the USOC 2000 National Coach of the Year for Table Tennis. I won it again in 2006, and was Developmental Coach of the Year in 1998.

Planning strategy between games at the 2000 Sydney Olympic Games Men's Doubles. Todd Sweeris hydrating and David Zhuang thinking.

Table Tennis Teen Leaps To No. 1 From 71st

BY CHARLIE VINCENT
Free Press Sports Writer

Danny Seemiller has one thing in common with most other 18-years-olds: He doesn't know quite how to handle fame.

Unlike most 18-year-olds he has the opportunity to try.

After six years of aimlessly drifting around among the nation's top 100 or so table tennis players, Seemiller decided to assert himself and quickly played himself into the No. 1 position on the United States team that will compete in the World Table Tennis Championships in Sarajevo, Yugoslavia, this spring.

Now he is not sure if he should brag about it . . . or maintain the veil of anonymity that surrounded him until he won the U.S. World Team tryouts in Chicago recently.

"TAKE MY picture over in the corner somewhere," he said Friday, motioning a photographer away from where several hundred players were competing in the U.S. Open Table Tennis Championships at Cobo Hall.

"Sports Illustrated did a story on me last week and it came out sounding like I was a real braggart," he explained. "I don't want my picture taken in front of all of the other players."

Seemiller was ranked 71st in the country before the Chicago tournament and he gives most of the credit for his quick rise to the coaching of Grand Rapids' Del Swerris, a veteran player and coach and one of the few U.S. players to defeat a member of the Chinese team during the historic tour of Red China.

"He invited me out to Grand Rapids to practice with him," the young Pittsburgher says, "and I've spent six or eight weeks working with him. It's been a tremendous help to my game."

That was evident in the Chicago meet, where he won 12 matches and lost just two — one of them to current U.S. champion Dal Joon Lee, who up until that time had never lost a match to a U.S. player.

"I'M NOT the only good young player," the mod-haired teenager points out. "There are a lot of good young players. But once they get out of high school they get interested in other things and don't work on their game. They just drop by the wayside."

He was determined that wasn't going to happen to him.

"When he graduated last June he came to us," Seemiller's father recalled. "And he said: 'Please don't push me into getting a job right away. I want to see how far I can go with this.'"

"We told him to go ahead and give it a try and his success in just the last six months has been amazing," the elder Seemiller admits.

It's been so amazing that Danny is talking serious about trying to make a living out of the sport.

"There are maybe four guys now who can live off table tennis," he says. "But that means there is a lot of opportunity. It's certainly not an over-crowded field.

"AFTER THIS tournament and the World Championships, I want to come back and open a club in Pittsburgh, where I can give lessons and exhibitions and things."

He has already played over 100 exhibitions.

Although his father has never played serious table tennis, the game began to interest Danny when he was 12. He began competing in local tournaments soon afterward, but

Please turn to Page 2D, Col. 7

No. 1 U.S. player Danny Seemiller prepares to slam or
Free Press Photos by JO

In 1972 I started to use anti-topspin on the free side of my paddle. Playing for four years without coaching, I developed a grip that became known as the "Seemiller Grip," where you use only one side of the paddle for forehand and backhand in a windshield-wiper way. Once I started to utilize the free side of my paddle, my ranking rocketed. The anti-topspin is a low friction, slow rubber that gave me a great change of pace and was helpful in returning serves.

Tip: It's important to try to have an all-around game since being able to adapt is one of the most important aspects of a player's game.

Si Wasserman, Hall Of Famer and USATT Lifetime Achievement award recipient, still plays regularly at 98 years old. Si has generously donated more than $250,000 to develop America's youth players.

Tip: Racket speed and friction are what causes spin. The more spin you can create on your shots the better the quality and consistency. Also, as a side product, you will recognize and read spin better and how to make adjustments.

PICKWICK INTERNATIONAL INVITATION TABLE TENNIS TOURNAMENT

Saturday 7th December 1974
Crystal Palace National Sports Centre

GROUP A	GROUP B
N. Bajaj	M. Orlowski
D. Neale	C. Barnes
N. Jarvis	E. Caetano
D. Seemiller	C. Pedersen

MR. PICKWICK

25p

I was invited to participate in the 1974 Pickwick Invitational. It was held at Crystal Palace. I have had many fond memories of competing in England and this was my first one in 1974. Nicky Jarvis, Ian Horsham and Albert Shipley were very helpful during my many trips as I often traveled alone.

"The Official Sydney 2000 Olympic Games – Opening Ceremony 15 September 2000"

The Opening Ceremony at the 2000 Sydney Games. Such a beautiful scene as 110,000 spectators cheered on the world's best athletes. Up front by the flagpole on the right there are many white hats. I am under one of them.

199

USA TABLE TENNIS NATIONAL CHAMPIONS

Year	Men's Singles	Women's Singles	Men's Doubles	Women's Doubles	Mixed Doubles
2015	Yijun Feng	Jiaqi Zheng	Yijun Feng/Jack Wang	Wang Chen/Ying Lu	Yijun Feng/Ying Lu
2014	Jimmy Butler	Lily Zhang	Cory Eider/Allen Wang	Lily Zhang/Jiaqi Zheng	Timothy Wang/Lily Zhang
2013	Timothy Wang	Ariel Hsing	Theodore Tran/Jeff Huang	Judy Hugh/Ariel Hsing	Timothy Wang/Ariel Hsing
2012	Timothy Wang	Lily Zhang	Timothy Wang/Han Xiao	Gao Jun/Erica Wu	Timothy Wang/Ariel Hsing
2011	Peter Li	Ariel Hsing	Timothy Wang/Han Xiao	Gao Jun/Erica Wu	Timothy Wang/Ariel Hsing
2010	Timothy Wang	Ariel Hsing	Ilija Lupulesku/Yiyong Fan	Jasna Reed/Judy Hugh	Adam Hugh/Judy Hugh
2009	Michael Landers	Gao Jun	Dan Seemiller/Mark Hazinski	Gao Jun/Crystal Huang	Liu Hui Yuan/Gao Jun
2008	David Zhuang	Crystal Huang	David Zhuang/Shao Yu	C. Huang/Tawny Banh	Samson Dubina/C.Huang
2007	Ilija Lupulesku	Wang Chen	Ilija Lupulesku/Mark Hazinski	Wang Chen/Judy Hugh	Han Xiao/Jackie Lee
2006	David Zhuang	Wang Chen	David Zhuang/Han Xiao	C. Huang/Tawny Banh	Mark Hazinski/C. Huang
2005	Ilija Lupulesku	Jasna Reed	Ilija Lupulesku/Mark Hazinski	C. Huang/Whitney Ping	Adam Hugh/Lily Yip
2004	Cheng Yinghua	Gao Jun	Ilija Lupulesku/Mark Hazinski	Gao Jun/Tawny Banh	Cheng Yinghua/Gao Jun
2003	Ilija Lupulesku	Jasna Reed	Ilija Lupulesku/David Zhuang	Jasna Reed/Tawny Banh	I. Lupulesku/Jasna Reed
2002	Ilija Lupulesku	Gao Jun	Cheng Yinghua/Han Xiao	Gao Jun/Jasna Reed	Sean O'Neill/Jackie Lee
2001	Eric Owens	Gao Jun	David Zhuang/Eric Owens	Gao Jun/Jasna Reed	Cheng Yinghua/Gao Jun
2000	David Zhuang	Gao Jun	David Zhuang/Todd Sweeris	Gao Jun/Michelle Do	Cheng Yinghua/Gao Jun
1999	Cheng Yinghua	Gao Jun	David Zhuang/Todd Sweeris	Gao Jun/Michelle Do	David Zhuang/Gao Jun
1998	David Zhuang	Gao Jun	Eric Owens/Barney Reed	Gao Jun/Virginia Sung	David Zhuang/Gao Jun
1997	Cheng Yinghua	Gao Jun	Cheng Yinghua/Jack Huang	Gao Jun/Amy Feng	Cheng Yinghua/Gao Jun
1996	Cheng Yinghua	Gao Jun	Cheng Yinghua/Todd Sweeris	Gao Jun/Amy Feng	Cheng Yinghua/Gao Jun
1995	David Zhuang	Amy Feng	Khoa Nguyen/Darko Rop	Wei Wang/Lily Yip	David Zhuang/Amy Feng
1994	David Zhuang	Amy Feng	David Zhuang/Dan Seemiller	Amy Feng/Lily Yip	David Zhuang/Amy Feng
1993	Jimmy Butler	Amy Feng	David Zhuang/Sean O'Neill	Amy Feng/Lily Yip	David Zhuang/Amy Feng
1992	Jimmy Butler	Amy Feng	David Zhuang/Sean O'Neill	Wei Wang/Lily Yip	David Zhuang/Amy Feng
1991	Sean O'Neill	Insook Bhushan	John Onifade/Dan Seemiller	I. Bhushan/Diana Gee	Sean O'Neill/Diana Gee
1990	Jimmy Butler	Wei Wang	Sean O'Neill/Dan Seemiller	I. Bhushan/Diana Gee	Sean O'Neill/Diana Gee
1989	Sean O'Neill	Insook Bhushan	Jimmy Butler/Scott Butler	I. Bhushan/Diana Gee	Brian Masters/I. Bhushan
1988	Sean O'Neill	Insook Bhushan	Eric Boggan/Sean O'Neill	I. Bhushan/Diana Gee	Dan Seemiller/I. Bhushan
1987	Sean O'Neill	Insook Bhushan	Quang Bui/Brian Masters	I. Bhushan/Diana Gee	Sean O'Neill/Diana Gee
1986	C. Teekaveerakit	Insook Bhushan	Sean O'Neill/H. Teekaveerakit	I. Bhushan/Diana Gee	Sean O'Neill/Diana Gee
1985	Sean O'Neill	Insook Bhushan	Quang Bui/Brian Masters	I. Bhushan/Diana Gee	Sean O'Neill/Diana Gee
1984	Eric Boggan	Julie Ou	Scott Boggan/P. Schwartzberg	Diana Gee/Lisa Gee	Quang Do/Lisa Gee
1983	Dan Seemiller	Insook Bhushan	Dan Seemiller/Rick Seemiller	I. Bhushan/Diana Gee	Dan Seemiller/I. Bhushan
1982	Dan Seemiller	Insook Bhushan	Dan Seemiller/Rick Seemiller	Jin Na/Angelita Rosal	Dan Seemiller/I. Bhushan
1981	Scott Boggan	Insook Bhushan	Dan Seemiller/Rick Seemiller	I. Bhushan/K. Dawidowicz	Dan Seemiller/I. Bhushan
1980	Dan Seemiller	He-Ja Lee	Dan Seemiller/Rick Seemiller	He-ja Lee/Angelita Rosal	R. Seemiller/C. Dadian
1979	Attila Malek	He-Ja Lee	Dan Seemiller/Rick Seemiller	He-ja Lee/Angelita Rosal	E. Boggan/K.Dawidowicz
1978	Eric Boggan	Insook Bhushan	Dan Seemiller/Rick Seemiller	He-ja Lee/Angelita Rosal	Dan Seemiller/I. Bhushan
1977	Dan Seemiller	Insook Bhushan	Dan Seemiller/Rick Seemiller	I. Bhushan/K. Dawidowicz	Dan Seemiller/I. Bhushan
1976	Dan Seemiller	He-Ja Lee	Dan Seemiller/Rick Seemiller	I. Bhushan/He-ja Lee	Dan Seemiller/I. Bhushan
1976	Ray Guillen				
1936	Sol Schiff				

Update (no Nationals in 2020 due to Covid)

Year	Men's Singles	Women's Singles	Men's Doubles	Women's Doubles	Mixed Doubles
2019	Kanak Jha	Lily Zhang	Kanak Jha/Yijun Feng	Crystal Wang/Amy Wang	Nikhil Kumar/Amy Wang
2018	Kanak Jha	Juan Liu	Kanak Jha/Krishnateja Avvari	Jian Liu/Xinyue Wang	Kanak Jha/Amy Wang
2017	Kanak Jha	Lily Zhang	Gal Alguetti/Sharon Alguetti	Wu Yue/Xinyue Wang	Wu Yue/Gao Yanjun
2016	Kanak Jha	Lily Zhang	Jeffrey Huang/Newman Cheng	Lily Zheng/Jiaqi Zheng	Yijun Feng/Jiaqi Zheng

A News Article from the _South Bend Tribune_ – Dec. 19, 2019

South Bend Table Tennis Star and Two-time Olympic Coach Takes His Own Swing at the Games

By Bill Moor

Dan Seemiller of New Carlisle is trying to make the 2020 U.S. Olympic team in table tennis.

He certainly has the kind of résumé that gives his quest more than a little credibility: a five-time national singles champion … once a Top 20 performer in the world … and even a two-time Olympic coach.

"Sometimes when I'm playing, I feel like I'm 18 again" Dan says. "But then, sometimes when I first get out of bed in the morning, I feel a little wobbly."

There's a reason for that. He's 65.

Old enough for Medicare. Old enough to get a senior discount anywhere he goes. And some might say, old enough to know better.

An Olympian? At 65? Is he kidding?

When Dan told his wife Valerie what he had in mind, she said, "Good luck."

He will need plenty of that to out-duel players less than half his age. But then remember, we're talking about Dan Seemiller, one of the greatest U.S. players of all time and a guy who knows the game better than just about anyone after coaching it for more than 40 years.

For those of you now a little confused about what table tennis is, think Ping-Pong. "I still like calling it Ping-Pong even though table tennis is the name of the sport," Dan says.

His own way of playing has a name, too. It's called the "Seemiller style" — the unique way he holds the paddle and how he uses it to vary his shots.

And that's his reason for thinking he can make the Olympic team. "Without my technique, I wouldn't have a chance," he admits. "But because I play a much different game than anyone else, I might be able to make a run."

He plays in a way that changes the depth of the game — whacking the ball one time and putting it barely over the net the next. While most top-ranked players are slammers, Dan is all about finesse — in and out, left and right, fast and slow.

"It's a little like a football team suddenly coming up against a wishbone offense," he says.

Dan is back in training and competing after spending the last 23 years as the coach of the South Bend Table Tennis Club, now located in the old Beacon Bowl. He has developed more than a handful of national junior team players, including his son Dan Jr., and has coached thousands of kids, including a couple of Adams High School juniors — Dion Payne-Miller and Marty Stoner — who could go places in the sport.

"My focus since 1996 has been taking my players to tourneys and running around and coaching them. So I've had to get back in good shape. Everything on me has ached at times. I don't think some people know how grueling table tennis can be."

Dan has a lot of supporters who have set up a GoFundMe account to help him in his travels to tournaments and the Olympic Trials in late February.

He already has had quite a journey in the sport he started playing with his five brothers while growing up in Pittsburgh. For a long time, table tennis was his second love. He was a second baseman in baseball and had a tryout with the hometown Pirates. He hoped to play in the major leagues at Three Rivers Stadium where he had sold cotton candy while in high school.

But as an 18-year-old, he was ranked 71st in the country at table tennis and caught the attention of top player Dell Sweeris. "I moved to Grand Rapids to serve as his practice partner," he says. "Six months later, I was ranked No. 1 and made the U.S. national team. Dell didn't."

It was all table tennis after that — a total of 24 national titles (in singles, doubles, and mixed doubles), a five-year run as the president of the U.S. Table Tennis Association and induction into the USA Table Tennis Hall of Fame in 1995.

In 1996, Dan pretty much retired from competitive playing and moved to South Bend to coach — maybe with one regret: He never played in the Olympics after table tennis became an Olympic sport in 1988 — when he was already 34.

Now he's 65 with a sore knee, a lack of speed and a quirky style. Don Quixote with a paddle.

Don't bet against him.

Other Books by Danny Seemiller

Whether you're a competitive tournament player or a serious recreational player, Winning Table Tennis: Skills, Drills, and Strategies will help you improve your game. Dan Seemiller, 5-time U.S. singles and 12-time doubles champion, shows you all the shots and strategies for top level play. This book features 19 drills for better shot-making, plus Seemiller's own grip and shot innovations that will give you an edge over the competition. Featuring the most effective table tennis techniques and strategies, *Winning Table Tennis* shows you how to:

- choose the right equipment,
- serve and return serves,
- use proper footwork and get into position,
- practice more efficiently,
- prepare for competitions,
- make effective strategy decisions in singles and doubles play,
- condition your body for optimal performance.

If you are in the sport of table tennis, then you know Danny Seemiller, USA's greatest modern champion. In "Revelations of a Table Tennis Champion," the five-time U.S. Men's Singles Champion takes you through his 50+ years in the sport, from the early days of training, the breakthroughs, the agonizing defeats, and the great triumphs. You'll learn why the three-sport star – baseball, basketball, and football – changed his focus to table tennis. You'll experience his trips around the world, from being marched at gunpoint to achieving his boyhood dream of defeating the Chinese. But playing is only half his story. Danny, a long-time coach first in Pittsburgh and then in South Bend, IN, was the U.S. Olympic and World Team Coach for ten years, and was named the USOC Coach of the Year for Table Tennis three times. He was president of USA Table Tennis for five years and ran dozens of major tournaments through the years, including a US Nationals. He is a member of the USA Table Tennis Hall of Fame, and in 2012 became the youngest recipient of the Lifetime Achievement Award. This is his story.

Made in United States
Orlando, FL
25 October 2022

23775657R10113